COLLEGIATE BATTLEFIELD

JEFF CONNORS, ms, mscc, rscc-e

ACKNOWLEDGEMENTS

I would first like to thank my wife, Michele for typing and re-typing my handwritten manuscript.

Secondly, I would like to recognize Major Jamie Farrelly USMC (Ret) for scheduling Marines to speak to our football team on leadership principles. I want to thank MSgt. John Dailey USMC (Ret) and Colonel George H. Bristol USMC (Ret) for their contributions. Finally, I would like to extend my appreciation to Bethany Bradsher for editing and Stephanie Dicken and Pirate Media LLC for graphic design.

DEDICATION

This book is dedicated to the 58,220 individuals who made the ultimate sacrifice in Vietnam. I remember when Richard Nixon's daughter got married on my fifteenth birthday. Nixon was struggling with the incredibly intense outcry to end this war. I had been watching daily news clips and coverage of the turmoil on our small black and white television. It had been raging on for many years. If the battle had continued, I might have been a casualty. The veterans of Vietnam not only endured the conflict but returned home to a climate of disrespect and violent protest. Those who were wounded and those that lost their lives lived by the same principles that remain highly valued by our current military organizations. We see these same principles brought to life as ingredients producing success in collegiate football. I salute those who fought to sustain the principles which are so vital to success of this country and so integral to the character of rising generations.

PREFACE

LEADER OF MEN
Colonel G. H. Bristol USMC (Retired)

My adult life has been about leading. I have done it in peacetime and I have done it in war. I have been honored to lead Soldiers, Sailors, Airmen, and Marines in combat a group of Pre-Kindergarten through High School at a Classical Christian School. I have had great leaders and some sub-standard leaders over me. My 38-plus years in the Marine Corps allowed me to see leaders of other cultures and nations under pressure. I feel pretty confident that I know something about what a good leader, a not-so-good leader, an evolving leader, and a GREAT leader is.

Jeff Connors is many things. He was an OBSESSED High School and College football player. He is one of our country's top-tier Strength and Conditioning Coaches. He is in a couple of Halls of Fame. He is a great husband, father, and friend. Though tested by the rigors of time, he is still a man who holds his own in a weight room with young men half his age. He is a devoted Christian; a scholar; and a man with deep convictions to young people and where our country is headed in this dynamic time.

But he is something else. Jeff Connors is a LEADER.

He breathes it, honors it, and lives it every day. Leading groups of athletes to become leaner, harder, stronger, and more functionally capable of performing at the apex of their God-given talent. Pushing young men harder to find the intangible aspects that make a great athlete: the combination of ability, potential, work ethic, and drive. Watching him in action, I am struck by the fact that this humble but extremely driven man could succeed in any chosen endeavor. His knowledge is vast. His dedication is deep and never ceasing. His compassion and care for those in his charge is inspiring. You don't hear Jeff Connors talking about how much he lifted or what he did. His entire ethos revolves around the athlete he is training in that workout; in that moment; in that set or complex of exercises. His raspy voice may be barking commands – but make no mistake about it: he is leading that man or group to overcome gravity, mental limitations, and inhibitions. Jeff has been there and done it himself. He KNOWS what it is to become the strongest and the fastest he can be – and he is LEADING young men each and every day to find more than bigger biceps or a new Max lift in the squat. He is leading them to find the inner drive that fosters the discovery of the will to succeed. Whether it leads to the NFL or simply the discovery of the fact that hard work produces a man of honor, pride, and commitment, each and every athlete touched by Jeff Connors has been led and mentored to look inside them and find what they can be. They are LED by a LEADER to compete in the game of LIFE.

We live in a time that in many ways leans away from competition of any type. I watch as "participation" trophies have become prevalent in sports and – shockingly – some youth leagues do not keep score so as to "not hurt anyone's feelings." Rather than lead young people to push themselves, an attitude of "it is okay to just be average" has pervaded society. Rather than develop leaders, there is a tendency to develop followers – and our drop in academics, athletics, and service to country is germane as an offshoot of this attitude.

From our beginnings as a British colony, the spirit of America was born in the form of leaders who stood up, took a stand or a cardinal direction, and proceeded. The Washingtons, Lincolns, Roosevelts, and Reagans of our heritage were men who were mentored as youths and young man and struck out with confidence and fortitude to stake their claim. I am a strong believer that competitive athletics build many of the characteristics of a good leader-in-the-making: drive, responsibility, teamwork, sportsmanship, and adjusting to being both the leader and the led at times during games and seasons.

Jeff Connors knows about being an athlete. He has felt the adulation of victory and the agony of defeat. His father was his coach – and he had a front row seat watching his role model lead and mentor young men along the path to adulthood. Jeff has had countless athletes enter his domain – the realm of Strength and Conditioning – and he has taught, pushed, mentored and LED each and every one of them. His office walls are adorned with athletes who have benefitted from his ethos, humanity, and high standards. I know Jeff personally and have seen him in action. The most rewarding thing about knowing him is this fact: if a young athlete wants to be better, he or she will get better for knowing and working with Jeff Connors. He will coach and lead a junior varsity athlete and an NFL player the exact same way: with honor, respect, and dedication. He would never ask them to do anything he would not do or has done himself.

He will not like the fact that I am telling this one – but I will anyway. In his garage, he has an evil squat machine. Squats – as any athlete knows – will test you physically and mentally. They are beneficial. They are also painful and have a way of becoming bigger-than-life in the minds of a competitive athlete. "Squat Day" is not one that young men wake up and say, "Oh this is going to be fun…"

I asked Jeff why he has that contraption in his garage. He works in a state-of-the-art facility and can use the motivation of working out in front of young guys to get himself a great workout. He has been an "Iron Man" for many years now – and when I asked him, he smiled.

"That machine is sitting there waiting for me and only me," he said, "Just like some of my boys (and he uses that term for his athletes a lot) dread coming to work out, and sometimes I dread coming home and knowing that I need to do it too. But I do." There are no mirrors; no fancy sound systems – just a man and some iron waiting to be squatted.

In my world, we have a saying about those in charge: leaders take care of Marines – Marines take care of the mission. But leaders have to lead from the front. Jeff Connors leads from the front.

For those of you getting ready to read this book, you are getting a glimpse into the mind and the method of a man who is at the elite level of his profession. You won't read a lot of "I did this or that" from him – but make no mistake, he is a master of his craft. You will learn about what it takes to succeed in taking already talented athletes and making them more capable, more focused, and infinitely tougher.

But if you look closer, you will see a man dedicated to providing our great nation with men who will become better citizens, better fathers, and better Americans. And yes, better leaders in a time where our country is crying out for young people to stand up and lead.

Jeff Connors is a friend of mine, so I am slightly biased. But I am 60 years old and have done my share of competing myself. I think I can say that he is a man to "ride the river with" in any weather. I applaud him for taking the time and the effort to write a book about leadership from his unique and "in the trenches" perspective. He puts his heart, soul, and body into everything he does – he knows of no other way.

I am proud to say I live in a country that produces a man and a leader of men like him. I pray that I always do.

Semper Fidelis!

George H. Bristol Colonel USMC (Retired)

Whitefish, Montana March 2018

Colonel George H. Bristol USMC (Retired) is a native of Rhode Island and enlisted in the United States Marine Corps in 1975 and served for 38 years as an enlisted Marine and Marine Officer in infantry, intelligence, and special operations. He commanded at every commissioned officer rank; served for 19 of his 38 years overseas; and served in over 64 months of combat operations in Afghanistan, Iraq, Somalia, and the Balkans. He is a lifetime martial artist who created the Marine Corps Martial Arts Program – an integrated fighting system that exists to the present day for all Marines. He lives in Whitefish, Montana.

INTRODUCTION

Through the last five decades I have been closely aligned with and dedicated to athletics, both as a coach and as a participant. I have always been someone who believes in the power of human emotion. For as long as I can remember, and within every level of competition and geographic location I have ever coached, the value of character and human spirit have been factored in and meshed with varying degrees of raw talent. The combination of these two elements forms the heart and potential of a team. We must talk about physical attributes and read countless articles and books concerning training methods, but we can also consider the human spirit as the true magic within a collegiate football team. I don't believe that you can ever talk about it enough. It is an effective life-giving principle.

Where an attitude is concerned, an animated individual is going to possess energy and an exceptional work ethic, as long as his passion is in the right place. Research first introduced in a 1993 *Psychology Review* article provides good news for coaches. The concept described in the research is referred to as "deliberate practice." This idea has been widely studied and referenced as somewhat of a new awakening to the power of a work ethic driven by a powerful spirit. Even more significant is the implication of the impact of the deliberate coach. Because it has been theorized that it takes 10 years or 10,000 hours of deliberate practice to reach one's potential, it would also indicate that one's potential would not be achieved without exceptional coaching. Coaches need to be relentless in staying on the cutting edge of their game, with the realization that they can impact individuals significantly during this 10-year process. They can reinforce the constructs of deliberate practice, which include a "pathological relentlessness," "constant self critique," and a "grinding commitment."

The current generation of young athletes has been questioned in many respects regarding commitment and feelings of entitlement, so much so that there has also been speculation as to whether they are truly willing to pay the price. Yet we continue to see world-class athletes exceeding the limits of the human body and setting new records, possibly resulting from the advances in current training. Similar to many other athletes of previous generations, I love to reminisce about how it was "back in the day." Yes sir, everything was tougher and as a result, so were we. The "junction boys" didn't have anything on us. Practice was frequent, long and brutal, and summer training was nothing short of a nightmare. We had to suffer at least one concussion a week.

Conditioning was nothing less than torturous, and we certainly were not afforded the luxuries of water. Unbuckling a chinstrap never even entered the conversation. There was severe punishment for mental mistakes and anything less than 100 percent effort. It was extreme boot camp mentality at its finest. Sometimes I have wondered why these are my fondest memories. Could it be that those rigorous and barbaric demands that we love to sentimentalize somehow express our personal history of self-perceived mental toughness? In fact, most of us believe the whole nation is softer today. I even heard a rumor that Parris Island was required to modify and tone down its previous standards.

The reality here is that even the midst of mild sarcasm these stories are barely exaggerated. I survived them and know them to be true. I will always be proud of the challenges that I was able to physically and mentally overcome, and they will continue to influence my expectations of others. I ask myself if the power of the human will was more prevalent in the past. Did we, in fact, achieve a higher level of performance because of the fanatical demand? Sometimes you have to wonder about the common phenomenon in collegiate football whereby clearly lesser teams on paper reign victorious over superior opponents, otherwise referred to as "upsets." Would a survey possibly discover that a few decades ago, when we had tougher standards and greater character, these occurred less frequently? We are quite certain that we are bigger, faster and stronger, but have the intangibles fallen behind the measurables?

I'm not sure if the current generation gives a flying flip about what happened in the memories of those of us who may have been concussed beyond accurate recollection. They are labeled as more concerned about numbers of Facebook likes and comments in a retweet. They have a modus operandi of narcissism and a limited desire for hard work. They need to know the "why" for every demand. They do not like to pay a high price to achieve a reward. I had a couple of these human beings living under my roof for many years, and can attest to a moderate level of truth to these allegations.

If I were to present any argument on behalf of this current generation, it would include statistics regarding the young people who have recently sacrificed life and limb to defend this country. Not long ago, I attended my son's boot camp graduation ceremony at Lackland Air Force Base in San Antonio. I believe that boot camp should be mandatory for all young Americans. The ceremonies were some of the most moving experiences I've ever witnessed relative to discipline and human spirit, and I've been part of some great wins in large stadiums packed with cheering fans. The first ceremony began with the streets lined with over a thousand parents watching sons and daughters run in formation with their units. Each unit had its own themed shirts and "Jody chant." It was a highly disciplined awards ceremony with an impressive array of flawless marching drills. The activities continued into the next day and culminated with a graduation ceremony conducted in an area the size of fifteen football fields surrounded by vintage war planes. Each unit marched by the General with machine-like precision as the Airmen turned and saluted in unison. There were 700 young men and women in this class. After they recited the

"Airman's Creed," ending with a booming, "and I will not fail!" I was almost knocked out of my chair by their collective spirit.

The finale was a mob of parents sprinting out to meet their sons or daughters. It gave me a whole new perspective toward all of the generalizations we hear regarding this generation. Other, more positive, observations of the millennials ring true too, such as the way they respond to mentorship and positive reinforcement. That day, they had toughness and spirit. The point here for me is you get what you demand. Sometimes I'm not convinced that this generation is much different than any other, and I blame the leadership. We have to find a way to deal with the negatives of social media, and fatherlessness seems to be at an all-time high. The number of single parent scenarios always appears staggering. If we expect to optimize the power of the human will as an ingredient to victory, we are going to have to be more deliberate in providing a higher level of education toward the heightened demands of authority at the collegiate level.

I am proposing an extensive orientation process that would last for several months. Athletes would learn, at a much deeper level, a method of surviving and thriving within the rigors of the student/athlete lifestyle. As we hope to develop a dynamic spirit within a team, a spirit that remains resilient and consistent, we must address problematic commonalities and equip our young athletes at a higher level. We must equip them to understand the demand. They must understand self-discipline as a bridge of trust. I once heard someone say that an "ounce of prevention is worth a pound of cure." We need to reexamine the process of adaptation to college life. I'm not proposing a soft approach by any means, but we need to attack the undisciplined mind and renew it.

We renew it with the culture and tradition of the program. We involve successful upperclassmen as examples and influences from within. We also teach values that are common to nationwide and worldwide success. These can be thought of as universal principles. It is also very important to understand the expectations of the NCAA. We need more direct interaction between NCAA representatives and the student athletes. If we are going to use the term "team chemistry," it needs to be more closely and specifically defined. It reflects the nature of the collective personality of a team. I prefer the term "perfect team chemistry" so that we can establish specific objectives around the strength of the components. The components that come together to form perfect team chemistry are a fanatical work ethic, a raging pursuit of the mastery of a specific demand , a relentless desire to identify and change weakness and a fierce competitive mentality.

Similar to the way we define chemistry, team chemistry is composed of the structure, properties and reaction of the substance. The substance is every team member. When the substance changes (the individual digresses from the four components of the team chemistry), success at the highest level becomes vulnerable. This vulnerability can be manifested through a number of expressions of behavior. These would include lack of focus, reduction in quality of effort, manufacturing of excuses, decline in leadership and seeking the easiest path toward mere compliance.

The following chapters will explore the gamut of the theories and training systems that I have been able to observe and experience throughout my personal athletic and coaching career. We never hear much about the strength and power of the human will. The only fully legitimized program directed specifically toward developing the human spirit is found within the training of the United States military organizations. These organizations have designed their training processes to get every ounce of sweat out of each recruit. The Marines refer to the human will as the "chief incalculable," and they proceed to make it calculable through the indoctrination of discipline and spirit. There are some strikingly similar parallels between the objectives of the military and collegiate football teams. The takeaways in terms of leadership, mentality, tempo and tradition are immeasurable.

Everything that I've observed thus far is that military organizations are well aware of the characteristics of our current young men and women, and they have still kept the standard of training very high. The 14 leadership qualities of the Marine Corps, for example, have not changed, and they certainly carry significant impact as a system of successful principles.

From a slightly different perspective, Brene Brown wrote a book entitled *Daring Greatly,* and within the book she cited a phenomenon called the Narcissistic Epidemic, discovered by Keith Campbell. In the book, Brown maintains that narcissistic personality disorder has more than doubled in the United States over the last ten years. She talks about our first inclination to "cut them all down to size." We quickly blame narcissists with an attitude of contempt, anger and judgment. Her contention is that the diagnosis that points to grandiose behavior and a need for admiration is underpinned by shame. Shame is the cause, and it can never be the cure.

From here, moving into the world of college football as we currently know it, the most glaring issue is undoubtedly fatherlessness. We know that the relationship between single parent families and crime is stronger than the relationship between race and crime or the relationship between low income and crime. I'm not sure of the exact number of athletes from single parent homes who were members of the teams I've been with over the last thirty years, but it is safely predicted at over fifty percent. That factor, combined with the influence of a celebrity culture and social media, can combine to form some negative issues. The key is that knowing the cause obviously helps in dictating the change.

Guiding the young, collegiate football player toward his physical, mental and spiritual potential requires a balanced approach. At one end of the spectrum we can revert back to the Vince Lombardi quote: "No amount of pain, suffering, self sacrifice or dedication is too great a price to pay for the ultimate victory." The "no amount of pain" part might not fly with the recent issues we've witnessed, such as sickle cell trait. We also cannot deny the fact that somewhere beneath the surface of today's young men, we discover the complexity of troublesome issues. The more serious concerns--such as drug usage, accountability and inefficient time management-- threaten the athlete's survival and propensity to graduate. Is Brene Brown on the money with her reference to shame? After thirty years and thousands of hours with these athletes, I would strongly agree that there are underlying perplexities that need to be individually defined and professionally dealt with. If we are truly "fishers of men," a higher level of education toward an organized plan of redemption should be instituted as a major chapter in the life of a freshman who is ill prepared to be smashed in the side of the head with the demands of collegiate football.

CHAPTER ONE
THE INTEGRAL NATURE OF TRUST

Trust has been referred to as the glue of life. It is the most essential ingredient in developing successful relationships, and it never exists without effective communication. The nature of effective communication that must be developed between a coach and an athlete is unique — it requires the coach to acquire a very high level of skill. It also requires the recognition of the fact that young athletes develop trust based upon their gamut—or possibly the gauntlet—of past experiences. Sometimes those past experiences reflect a history of distrust, and the coach must be able to identify and address this characteristic early and effectively with those individuals.

When a young athlete enters a program, he is immediately faced with mental and physical challenges. All of us who played collegiate football at some level can remember the drastic attrition that occurred within that group of faces we first saw at freshmen reporting date. Many hit the bus station that first week, while others eventually fell by the wayside for various other reasons.

Decades ago when guys like me reported to camp, we expected to see the wheat separated from the chaff as the slackers were eliminated in immediate fashion. I can't remember many coaches being overly concerned about whether or not you trusted them. Of course, we had no restrictions on the number of individuals who reported to camp, except for the number of available helmets and shoulder pads. Three practices a day in the heat of summer tended to eliminate those individuals with a marginal commitment relatively quickly. There were no rules regulating your hourly commitment, weekly time commitment, or number of practices. Things have certainly changed.

I personally believe that the changes have presented a radical cry for

the development of mutual trust between the coach and athlete. Coaches need to be tuned into strategies that insure that elite athletes maintain a high level of effort and commitment. When you consider the number of coaches

Leading an incredible group of men through team flex in 1991. They would go on to be 11-1 and ranked 9th in the country.

some athletes have had through their careers, whether it be position coaches or head coaches, it is easy to understand how their level of trust begins to waiver. On the other hand, I've seen situations where a team believed that change was favorable. Not surprisingly, that sentiment was related to trust.

Developing Trust Between Coaches and Athletes

There are multiple models of developing trust. Most of these models originate in the corporate world, but in some instances they can be fundamentally applied to the coach-athlete relationship. Coaches often consider themselves individuals who serve others, and a servant leadership model could be as appropriate in the locker room as it has become in the corporate board room. But would it make sense to provide a collaborative atmosphere to young athletes who have just graduated from high school, some of whom have yet to even hold down any type of employment? Probably not.

The first quality of the servant leadership developed by CEO and business thought leader Skip Prichard is to value diverse opinions. There are probably a number of athletes within a program who have proven themselves responsible, earned trust and have become seasoned over time. Some will no doubt prove themselves impressive as vocal leaders, and coaches will look toward them to be team captains. I believe that there are times when as coaches we can value their opinions. We might even make subtle changes based upon their voices if we feel that their input is significant. Other components of the servant leadership approach that might warrant consideration are encouragement and helping people with life issues.

When you coach at the collegiate level, you quickly learn that almost every athlete requires some level of assistance with life issues. As previously mentioned, it is well established that many of today's athletes are fatherless. That doesn't necessarily indicate that they will somehow fail; they probably would not have made it to the collegiate scholarship level if failure was inevitable. Another strong figure in their life will certainly contribute to a positive future. A 1994 study by McCall and Land indicated that the family structure index is a strong predictor of suicide among young adult white males. Fortunately I've never witnessed anything like that firsthand, but if true it certainly underscores the need for encouragement.

I have been witness to and directly in the middle of countless incidences of what I might refer to as confusion toward authoritarian expectations. As much as I would like to encourage and serve our athletes, I am also aware of the dire need they have for strong, unwavering guidance and direction. As we consider an effective leadership style for the collegiate athlete, I advocate for a mix of military and servant leadership, with a hard emphasis on the military side. Military organizations talk about obedience, loyalty, respect and cooperation. They influence individuals to work with a high level of effort and overcome an array of challenges.

When you study organizations, there is much written about "shared vision." Let me share my thoughts about that lofty objective for a moment. I'm not attempting to be pessimistic in any manner, and I believe that when things are going well it indicates that the vast majority of individuals are on board. I personally believe that a front runner mentality is common today, particularly if a team does not achieve success early in a season. Losing games can magnify small issues and begin to establish a climate of doubt and an avalanche of excuses. The trust factor can be easily fragmented if individuals do not experience some degree of early success.

Bill Parcells stated that "confidence is born of demonstrated ability," and I believe that statement is so true. If you have individuals in your organization who demonstrate a fragile sense of character, problems will be inevitable. People outside the program really have no clue about the impact of character issues on a team. The Marines see character as the link between values and behavior. I could write fifty pages on that idea alone. I believe very strongly that if a young man has a strong passion for the game, a coach can continue to build his character. The player will listen because he wants to perform well. Many times he can recognize the connection. If you have three or four players out of a hundred who don't do the right things—like being where they are suppose to be and doing what they are supposed to be doing—you have distractions. Let's be very specific here. Since I entered collegiate coaching in 1988 I have seen dozens, and then more dozens, of player issues. Many of those situations never reach the public, and they shouldn't, but nonetheless they cause friction within the program.

Eliminating Friction

Military organizations talk about friction. Friction is prominent on the list of obstacles you might have to overcome to be successful. Here is where I might go to any extreme to make a point. This might seem rigid, but I strongly believe that even in the year 2018, you cannot allow any, and I mean zero friction, to exist on your team. Friction will raise its ugly head on a daily basis, and it's one hell of a lot easier for a position coach to ignore it and go about his business—breaking down film, studying the recruiting board, or talking to the media. But if I know anything about this insane business after thirty years, it is that you must attack and eliminate it.

The removal of friction needs to be your first priority. Every head coach I've worked for over the years has had to deal with it. Some have been unaware of the negative impact within their program, and others have been keenly "in tune." Even if you as a head coach are "in tune," you must have the willingness to act. You have to decide if you are going to compromise the standards of the program to preserve perceived talent. The reason I use the word perceived is because I believe that poor character erodes and hampers talent. Poor character or lack of effort, accountability, or spirit is friction. If you want a smooth program, someone is going to need to grind the friction into dust. I'm always happy to volunteer.

At one of the universities where I previously coached, I was assigned to be on the infractions committee. There were weeks where the infractions totaled around 70. That is some serious friction within a program. The sad thing is that the problem is usually self-induced. It should be enough to take on the degree of challenges outside of the organization, such as the teams on your schedule. In other words, focus on the mission. Self-induced friction interferes with the plan to complete the mission, and it can create internal disaster.

The other type of friction is totally different; it has little to do with trust, but it is worth mentioning as a necessary component within a team's preparation. If a team wants to be adequately prepared for competition, it must experience the same type of friction during practice that will occur on game day. There are various approaches out there to "game week" preparation. Coaches must strike a balance between "live" preparation in full pads and days spent in shells or shorts and a helmet. One of the best examples of specific preparation is when you face an option team.

Option teams are uncommon in many respects, and to prepare for one your defense is going to need as many practice repetitions as possible and a deep focus on live cut blocks. Unfortunately, I've had to stand on the sideline and witness the same cluelessness toward this specific type of offense several times over the years. If you can't adjust to eliminate the various threats that the option system presents, you are in deep trouble. The Marines refer to this type of resolution to specific problems as "tactical ability." Tactical ability calls for a unique solution. It requires both knowledge and judgment. Coaches need deep knowledge of the option system to defend it, and their limited ability to readjust to the game day adjustments of the competition spells defeat.

In a perfect world, we would like to think that we can recruit individuals who are going to make good decisions, adhere to team and NCAA rules and certainly avoid criminal activity. Unfortunately, the reality is that I have never experienced an extended period of time in any program without witnessing a frequent number of team issues. It comes down to this: Even though you may not trust a few individuals at a high level, you still are required to coach them. If they are talented and your team is marginally successful, you will probably have to tolerate them. That is never a good situation, particularly for the strength and conditioning coach. I believe that coaches have to immediately confront the "little things" and micro-manage every individual because they have uniquely different issues. Unfortunately, when you get away from that you have the beginning of friction. The only good news about the concerns toward these issues is that they usually exist within a minority. Everyone is familiar with the 10-80-10 theory, and in my experience in athletic programs it is definitely accurate.

Eliminating Trust Busters

Trust has to flow in both directions, so it is important to identify the trust busters that cause high character individuals to go south. I believe that playing time, or more specifically a lack thereof, can impact the very best aspiring young athlete. I've seen a drastic demeanor change in a number of athletes because of progressive disappointment with their perceived role in the program. They often fail to believe that everyone has been truthful with them, and when their position coach is changed frequently the issue gets worse. Athletes who have a higher level of trust toward their coaches are more likely to have a consistently positive demeanor. Athletes usually just want to hear the truth about their status.

We had a running back at UNC who was moved to defense early in his career. He was moved under the regime that had recruited him. Of course, the expectation is always to be willing to sacrifice for the team. I experienced it during my own collegiate career. My coach met with me and explained that I would be moving from quarterback to defensive back for the good of the cause. I had started at quarterback the previous season after a redshirt year. My attitude was very positive, because the way he communicated it to me made me feel that I had a high level of physicality and that I would better serve the program in another position. I was happy that he recognized that I was wiling to hit people.

I didn't know much about the explanation that was given to our running back at UNC, but he and his parents seemed to be miserable with the situation. His performance as a defensive back was mediocre. After a period of time a regime change took place. He was moved back to running back, and the bottom line is that he currently remains a running back in the NFL six years after graduation. I don't think that good coaches make many mistakes where the best use of personnel is concerned, but this particular case went as far as impacting team morale. Sometimes coaches need to go the extra mile to educate players about their individual roles in the program.

When a young athlete enters a collegiate football program he is becoming set in his ways of thinking, but hopefully the cement is still wet. I had an opportunity to coach high school in Florida for six years, and I really hated the poverty level income. I lived paycheck to paycheck with only a bed in my rented apartment. I was getting crushed financially, but I truly enjoyed the appreciation level from the athletes and parents. It is hard to put a price tag on the feeling that you are the source of positive influence. The recent movement toward establishing full time strength and conditioning coaches at the high school level is going to have a significant impact toward a higher level of physical and mental preparation at that level. It is a great development.

I had a rewarding experience with a small group of young men at a small 1-A private school.

The year I got hired, the school was going to drop wrestling because of a lack of interest. I was asked if I would take the program and attempt to revive it. There were essentially no other small schools in Palm Beach County, so we would have to wrestle all 4 and 5-A schools or travel. The first year, with a team of nine underclassmen, we won no matches. The second year, after recruiting fifteen more athletes to come out for wrestling and attend summer camp at Clemson, our team ended winning ten dual matches, and over the next three seasons we defeated large schools such as Boca Raton, Palm Beach Gardens and Jupiter. It was an incredible period of overachievement. My coaching approach was as basic as dirt. I played football in college and I hadn't wrestled since high school. We won because of character and trust. Of course, we conditioned beyond what anyone else was doing. That never hurts.

I'm going to reiterate again, at this point, the importance of spending time with each individual athlete. When I was coaching that wrestling team, I taught five different history preps and had a chance to see the athletes throughout the day. There were always opportunities to meet with them outside of practice. I always knew about issues, because it was a small place with news traveling fast. Knowing your athletes is crucial, since they each have an individual set of issues. Because of my own experiences, I will continue to support any future effort to educate incoming freshmen at a higher level in a collegiate program. We desperately need an early and deliberate plan of earning trust.

Troubling Behavior That Damages Trust

I am also going to continue to emphasize and reemphasize the behavior, that I continue to witness, that prevents a team from reaching an attainable level of success. In my opinion, the most evident recurring issue is immaturity. I have dealt with some of the largest human beings on the planet who are nonetheless deficient in maturity. The immaturity factor repeatedly raises its ugly head on the lists of accountability within the program. Specifically, that list of those lacking in accountability includes issues with class, study hall, tutoring, treatment, losing issued equipment, and more. Maybe this sounds old school, but if I'm a position coach I'm trying to run my whole position group into the next world if one guy breathes wrong. That guy is going to feel serious pressure from his peer group. Wait, I'm neglecting the fact that we need to ask ourselves some important questions here. Does a trainer have to be present? Can physical activity be used as a punitive option? What if one of my guys says his ankle hurts? Does this activity fall within the weekly NCAA time requirements? The bottom line is that people have to grow up and become accountable, and the system seems to be moving in an opposite direction. I hope it doesn't affect the United States of America.

Probably the second most frequent issue is the way the highly talented athlete views himself. This individual has been courted through high school and the recruiting process because he is incredibly gifted. Sometimes there seems to be a correlation between giftedness and narcissism. The highly gifted individual is also idolized on social media, which further serves to convince them of their greatness. This problem has actually been around for as long as I can remember, even if social media is relatively new. Let me say again that some head coaches don't permit these attitudes to exist, confronting them at every turn. Others might provide lip service and count on someone else to handle it, while others may be on their last leg attempting to save their job and feel like they can't afford to lose talent. Anything less than total control is not going to go well for the future. It is painful to get rid of anyone you broke your back to recruit and bring into the program. And, what about the Academic Progress Rate? *"The Academic Progress Rate (APR) holds institutions accountable for the academic progress of their student-athletes through a team-based metric that accounts for the eligibility and retention of each student-athlete for each academic term. The APR system includes rewards for superior academic performance and penalties for teams that do not achieve certain academic benchmarks. Data are collected annually, and results are announced in the spring."*

This is just further justification for having an intense educational process in place as exceptional high school athletes enter the program.

Maturity and narcissism are not violations of NCAA rules. But marijuana consumption is a definite violation, regardless of the state in which you reside. Collegiate and high school athletes model themselves after what they see in the NFL. Mike Bianchi of the *Orlando Sentinel* published an amazing report in 2015. He referenced in his article that 50 to 60 percent of NFL players use marijuana, while nearly one-third of college athletes said they had smoked pot at least once in a 12-month period, according to the latest NCAA research. NFL athletes evidently see it as a means to recover and a better alternative than opiate pain killers. Really?

Bianchi also stated in his report that former Atlanta running back Jamal Anderson told Bleacher Report that 60 percent marijuana use was bare minimum throughout the league. Now I can tell you that in 1978, at a time where there was no testing, I was of the opinion that my teammates who indulged on a daily basis seemed to be temporarily lethargic and progressively apathetic. Just an observation. Bianchi also referenced Dr. Julian Bates, who stated that long term use could have detrimental effects on the brain. Let's reiterate again that it is illegal under federal law for marijuana to be consumed on college campuses, and it is against NCAA rules.

The issue of trust is the most damaging and the most troublesome. If athletes test positive for drug use and have to be suspended or dismissed, the perception of stability and discipline within a program is called into question. Sometimes it's not just perception, it's reality. Imagine that you're rolling along as a coach and suddenly four or five starters are suspended. I have experienced it firsthand. The program had a big win. The athletes went out and celebrated. Someone in the department decided it was the perfect time to "nail" somebody with an "in house" test. Of course, this would also suggest that the coach was losing team discipline. Did they deserve to be nailed? Absolutely. Tough decision.

This issue becomes extremely complex as far as some individuals are concerned. Institutional policy, of course, varies from program to program. Do you believe that using marijuana is an uncontrollable addiction? Do you believe that your team will smoke it, whatever the consequence? Did you smoke it yourself as a collegiate athlete and justify those actions by telling yourself it was better than alcohol abuse? The answers to these questions could influence the institutional policy, based upon nature of those who put it in place. Things are definitely moving in a frightening direction. Since those five guys got nailed, more lenient policies are now in place. The first offense might be counseling. The second offense might be a brief suspension. The third or fourth offense may dictate the end of a football career. Is it really worth it, in the whole scheme of your future? Wouldn't cold beer be a better alternative?

I believe that the next issue we witness on a frequent basis is poor effort. Again, it is not in the majority, but it exists. A substandard effort can become contagious. A lack of effort from one player is friction, and a tolerance for excuses can also become a huge problem. People who don't like to work can find a whole list of excuses. They run to the training room and devise intricate plans to work the system. Often these individuals don't care if they ever play the game; they are searching for a free ride. You are making yourself cross-eyed studying the depth chart, and they are devising a scheme to become a ghost. As soon as one physical ailment is resolved, another quickly replaces it.

Creating the Right Atmosphere

I believe that clarity is a vital component of achievement. Let's swing back to the responsibilities of the coach in establishing trust. I have used a phrase over the years very frequently. It goes like this: "Bring it up for information." I like to divide the daily program into segments, and prior to each segment I inform everyone in a very detailed manner what we are about to do. Young people like to know the "why" for everything they do. That is exactly what I provide to them, and then they have the opportunity to ask questions. It is incredible to me that people may not understand what you perceive to be very simple. Clarity, however, provides production and also establishes trust. Clarity is an indication of knowledge from those who provide it. If you have no objection to the task because you recognize the value, you get the job done.

Another strategy toward establishing trust is effective modeling. Expression, tone of voice and the way in which concepts and cues are conveyed might seem to be somewhat unimportant in the total scheme of communication. The truth is that many elite athletes learn more easily from modeling and visual cueing. Live video and visual cueing can shorten the learning curve in teaching advanced movement drills or complex exercises. The goal is to optimize the delivery and provide your athletes with the best opportunity for positive results. Results promote trust. When athletes recognize the fruits of their labor, they tend to respond favorably.

Steven Covey set forth thirteen behaviors that create an enrichment of trust. We can relate these to the experience of the collegiate athlete and assess character in the process. Primarily, these behaviors can serve as a guideline for coaches and players to collaborate and build positive relationships. On the coach's side, we can consider talking about creating transparency, clarity toward expectations, listening first, and extending trust. The athlete should demonstrate respect, show loyalty, deliver results, get better, confront reality, practice accountability, keep commitments and also extend trust. Many of these behaviors can be exhibited on both sides. The one that is probably the most important and not mentioned is to right wrongs—to admit and correct mistakes. Everybody makes them.

The most significant experience I've had in collegiate athletics concerning trust was during my first year at East Carolina University. Our football team was talented but had a wide variety of talent levels and personalities. Linebacker Robert Jones was a first-round draft choice, and quarterback Jeff Blake would enjoy a notable career in the NFL. Our noseguard and the other starting inside defensive lineman both weighed 241 pounds. We had an NFL-caliber safety and some other defensive backs that were starters with average speed. One of the best receivers that year was a walk-on, and several of our offensive linemen were not what you might refer to as the perfect body type for the position they played. The inside linebacker who played next to Robert Jones was a young man named Kenny Burnette, a very smart player with a high level of toughness who would not be considered a "fast twitch" athlete. The starting tailback probably ran a 4.7 forty-yard dash.

When I got my training groups organized and started to spend time with these guys and learn more about them, it was evident that they had a common thread of positive energy and a great attitude. One of the early observations about this team was that they very clearly trusted each other. They would end that season with eleven wins and a top ten ranking. If you looked at each position individually and graded the talent, the average grade would not have been equated with a top ten national ranking.

The two previous seasons had been very average, but Coach Bill Lewis had taken over the program with a very deliberate plan. He was running a tight ship, conducting extremely long and physical practices, and he had hired a group of rock star coaches who were very demanding of their position groups. Things seemed to be very demanding, and when I arrived I jumped right in with the program and the standard of expectation.

Summer training camp was brutal. We conditioned every day after practice, a routine which today seems to have become obsolete. Even though it was quite some time ago, I can still recall the culture of the program and the climate of every practice. What I remember more than anything, though, was the level of trust. We won some significant games early in the season that established a strong sense of unity. The players trusted the head coach and the offensive and defensive scheme. The coaches recognized that these guys wanted to win and were willing to play extremely hard for four quarters to make it happen. One victory built toward the next, and the fan base was rabid. Winning helps in breeding positive relationships, but the investment that was made in establishing a trusting culture was clearly evident.

Each one of these behaviors can be explored in great detail. Where collegiate football is concerned, I feel that there are some very specific questions that an athlete must answer in the affirmative to demonstrate that he is earning trust.

1. Do I go to class?
2. Do I go to study hall?
3. Do I show up for my tutors?
4. Do I give 100 percent effort at all times?
5. Do I show up on time?
6. Do I refrain from smoking marijuana or engage in any other illegal activity?
7. Am I committed to being the very best athlete I can be?
8. Do I exhibit passion, spirit and enthusiasm?
9. Do I provide respect to those who teach and coach me?
10. Can I define integrity and discipline?
11. Do I love the challenges and the grind of being a participant in collegiate football?
12. Am I a positive influence on my teammates?

Providing the right answers to these questions should earn you a ton of respect with your coaches and include you as an individual who models Covey's behaviors. Your coach will be prepared to provide all of the favorable answers to the many questions asked repeatedly by NFL scouts. If being considered for the NFL doesn't motivate you, you should do the whole world a favor and find some friends who feel like it's OK to lose, because you have a loser mentality.

In summary, I cannot emphasize enough that a willingness to establish mutual trust is a by-product of the powerful meaning of two words—loyalty and passion. Where I grew up, if you weren't loyal, somebody was kicking your ass. Real simple.

3rd Platoon 1st Force Reconnaissance Company, USMC preparing to launch from ship to conduct a Direct-Action Raid 1995.

"Gung-Ho"

By John Dailey

The Marine Raiders of World War II were America's first special operations force. They were created to strike back following the surprise attack on Pearl Harbor. For the men of the 2nd Marine Raider Battalion under the command of Col. Evans Carlson, training meant harsh conditions, little chow, and long hours marching with heavy packs. During their short but illustrious existence they conducted one of the first offensive operations of the war, landing on Makin Island in small rubber boats launched from submarines to take the Japanese garrison by surprise, then fighting valiantly through the Pacific Islands.

When these men were selected for the unit, they were issued a rifle, a knife, and an eight-foot length of rope. The rope had an eyelet woven into one end and a wooden toggle on the other. With these ropes one man could connect his toggle to the eyelet of the next man, and together they could use the constructed rope to scale any obstacle in their path.

This meant no one man had to carry a heavy rope—no one man was responsible for the progress of the unit. It also meant that each man was responsible to his teammates for keeping his rope secure, prepared, and ready to lend its length at any time to accomplish team objectives. This meant that each man not only do his share, but trust completely in the man to his left and right to do the same.

Under Carlson, the 2nd Raider Battalion developed the concept of "Gung-Ho." Taken from the Chinese words "Gông"—Work and "Hè" — Together. This concept was a radical departure from military norms at the outset of World War II, because it brought with it a new idea: leadership doesn't come with privileges, only responsibilities. In the Raiders, officers ate last, they carried their own loads, and they were expected to listen to the ideas and concerns of their men. Carlson recognized that in order to earn trust, you have to be willing to give it and you have to do the things necessary to prove yourself worthy of that trust.

Nowhere is trust more critical than on a small team in which every man depends on the guy to his left and right. I can't be worried that the man next to me isn't going to do his job because if I'm worried about him, I'm not laser focused on my own job. In this way, and only in this way, can small, highly trained teams achieve results that far exceed the sum of their parts.

JEFF CONNORS

CHAPTER TWO

THE POWER OF MENTAL AND PHYSICAL TOUGHNESS

Mental toughness seems to be a very deep topic, judging from the relevant publications recently available. Some individuals are relating the concept to the corporate world. Others view it as very specific to what someone aspires to achieve. Some even have meshed mental toughness with softer characteristics, such as compassion and creativity. People ask themselves if it actually exists. Is it learned? Is it simply an insatiable desire to succeed, whatever the goal?

Personally, I think that each of us has our own story and most human beings have been conditioned to have some level of mental toughness and resiliency. As you live your life, you will inevitably lose family and friends. Some go peacefully and some go tragically. Whatever the case, losing loved ones is very painful. You have to be tough to bury people, maintain your faith and carry on with your life. People who lose children don't continue through life without incredible resolve. Losing a job and experiencing a divorce are also very tough experiences. The last time I checked, there seemed to be quite a large number of individuals experiencing these disappointments as well. It seems like our lives were designed to experience events that force us to be mentally tough. Some people don't make it. They can't recover. Faith is vital.

The first time I thought about mental toughness, I was hearing stories about coal miners as a young boy. Both my grandfathers were coal miners in Western Pennsylvania for a grand total of exactly 100

years. All you had to do was look at what miners looked like when they came home from work, covered in coal dust, and you knew that there was a high degree of mental toughness involved in the daily occupation. Accidents, involving serious injury or death, were frequent. The wages were low, and miner strikes were brutal. As far as I was concerned as I was growing up, there were tough people around me all of the time. Wives of coal miners had to be equally tough, because they had to plan for that possible day when their husbands might not make it home.

Helping get the Pirates ready for the 1995 Liberty Bowl. Another group of tremendous young men who would defeat Stanford.

I believe that the mentality of a community can have a major impact on high school and collegiate athletics. I believe it because I experienced it. Anyone who grew up in Western Pennsylvania through the many decades when coal and steel were thriving also believes it and takes pride in it to this day. I promise you.

I have read about other places around the country where a similar mentality has existed. People work hard, and they want to see their children play the game of football hard. There is a tradition of mental toughness that then becomes an expectation. The other characteristic evident in these kinds of places is overachievement. Human stature and talent are great, but without the mental toughness to go with them individuals often fall short.

I've witnessed individuals who end up making the NFL rosters more as a result of a relentless mentality than talent. In fact, my perspective over the years has changed significantly because of the unexpected accomplishments of overachievers that I've had the privilege to coach. Sometimes the athletes themselves don't understand how far they can go. Some who possess the mental toughness to be relentless day in and day out accomplish great things because of that sheer mentality.

Personal Testing and Toughness

I recently had a life-changing experience that taught me, at age 60, a valuable lesson in mental toughness. It was characterized by a sense of irony, in that for a period of time God rained down a heavy shower of favor upon me that could be described as a bucket list of blessings followed by a lightning bolt to the right side of my head to test my humility.

After many years of being estranged from my daughter from my first marriage, I received a phone call that began a renewal of our father-daughter relationship. It was wonderful—something I had been praying for over many years. Next my other daughter, who had been diagnosed with an illness, started to make tremendous strides toward stability. This was also a significant blessing.

My parents had retired to Florida from Pennsylvania, and even though they had a very nice situation for many years they were beginning to fail. We were able to sell their house and move them two miles away from us where we could look out for them, and this was a huge relief for the whole family.

I got a phone call around that time from Chuck Stiggins, the executive director of the Collegiate Strength and Conditioning Association. He informed me that I would be soon inducted into the USA Strength and Conditioning Coaches Hall of Fame. That was totally unexpected, and it really made me appreciate life even more because I don't network much at all.

This barrage wasn't over yet. Shortly after that, I was nominated for the National Collegiate Strength Coach of the Year for the third time. Several weeks later, I was informed by the National Strength and Conditioning Association that I won the award. Now I began to become concerned. I started to drive defensively and not walk under any ladders.

My wife and I traveled to the national conference in Nashville, Tennessee to receive the award. It was a very nice ceremony followed by a few days of weather delay, but we finally made it home. The next day I got a phone call from my doctor informing me of results of a test I had undergone recently. The results showed a malignant melanoma, and doctors would have to take a sizable amount of tissue from the right side of my forehead. In addition, they couldn't determine if it had traveled into my lymph system, so I would need surgery to map the related lymph nodes, then remove and examine them. God punched me right in my face.

I was in denial about the seriousness of my diagnosis until the nurse told me it could travel through my body and take my life. I conducted some research and discovered that it was projected that in 2017 160,000 people would be diagnosed with melanomas, and 87,000 would go to stage 3.

I needed to meet with an oncologist to schedule my surgery. Ironically I had been serving on the Board of Directors for Riley's Army, an organization that raises money and serves area families going through cancer diagnosis and treatment with their children. Now I was a cancer patient. It was a shocking realization.

When I pulled into the visitor parking lot of the cancer center to meet with the oncologist I noticed it was full. I ended up talking with the valet, and he gave me a pass to park in the patient parking lot. He told me it was good for a year. I didn't want to hear that, and I wanted to scream at the guy. I wanted it rip it up and drive straight out of there. I might have done that if my wife wasn't meeting me there.

As I sat in the waiting room of the Leo Jenkins Cancer Center with forty other patients, I realized that my little wife's strength was now the strength coach's strength. I felt internally feeble as I looked around the room. This was a very serious place. I could only think of God's mercy and His healing power, and I wondered how many of these forty people would be healed and how many would be moving on to another place. I thought about my life and wondered how I might be considered worthy of His mercy. I had so many chances to be like Christ in my life, but many times I failed miserably. I could only think that I was being sent to the valley of humility to see if I had the strength and discipline to climb to the height of exceptional character.

The meeting with the oncologist was straight forward. It was unknown at this time if the cancer had spread. I would have to wait seven days for the surgery to biopsy my lymph nodes, and then up to another week or two to for the results. You start to sink deep within yourself. You had experienced other disappointments through life that felt like they might have hit the bottom of your soul, but this smashes right through it. I stopped and thought to myself that I now understand how those parents with children diagnosed with cancer feel everyday. The child's suffering is their suffering. I was moving into a deep state of mental suffering and tried hard not to admit to myself and certainly keep it hidden from the rest of the world

At that time I read an excerpt from a book that I picked up entitled "The Road to Character" by David Brooks. On page 94 it stated that "suffering opens up ancient places of hidden pain. It exposes frightening experiences that had been repressed, shameful wrongs that had been committed. It spurs some people to painfully and carefully examine the basement of their own soul. But it also presents the pleasurable sensation that one is getting closer to the truth."

Coming to terms with the truth about yourself requires a measure of mental toughness from within. You can't change if you don't face who you are. It is a self confession. It is the deepest form of humility. You have no choice in the matter. When you finally see that you are not invincible no matter what you've accomplished in this world, you will talk to yourself about who you are and finally begin to understand the journey toward the gold standard of integrity.-

#Chuckstrong

Another excellent point that Brooks alludes to is that an individual will need help from family and friends to achieve redemption. I coached with Chuck Pagano at ECU and UNC. He was then the head coach of the Indianapolis Colts. When Chuck was in his mid-thirties he had an issue with his health. After accepting the job with the Colts, he was diagnosed with leukemia. I noticed a change in him following that experience. #ChuckStrong became a nationally recognized effort to help him become cancer free. He battled with unwavering faith and defeated the disease.

When I learned of my melanoma I texted him, "I have a malignant melanoma. Checking my lymph nodes this week for precaution. Pray for me."

Chuck said: "Jeremiah 29:11. I will battle for you on my knees. Trust his plan."

I said, "I know your prayers are heard. God punched me in the mouth and I must respond. I never knew how your life changes in a moment."

Chuck said: "Mindset. Live in vision, not circumstances. He has equipped you for anything. #ConnorsStrong"

Approximately a week later, I received the results indicating that my lymph nodes were clear. All my senses were sharpened that day. I heard the birds singing. I felt the wind on my face. The sky was very blue. My wife's face looked angelic. Of course mental toughness also crossed my mind! I learned more about myself. I had adapted to the situation. I had progressed from a state of denial to one of faith. I attribute that to a life of maintaining a positive spirit, whatever the circumstances.

It seems somewhat insignificant, but I have a very intense fear of tight places and not being able to breathe — claustrophobia magnified times ten. MRIs terrify me. Earlier I expressed this to those who tested and prepared me for surgery. They lied to me about a scan I would have to endure on my head. The bottom line is that they tied my arms and legs down and put me in the tightest scanner in the universe, with my face an inch from the machine. Then they shut the lights out, told me not to move and kept me there for 45 minutes. I pretended I was somewhere else and devised a slow breathing system where I would equate 22 deep breaths with three minutes time. I'm sure a lot of people would have no problem with that situation, but all I can say is that when your life is threatened, you just get it done.

I kept texting Chuck.

I said: "Test negative. Not in my lymph system. Thanks for your prayers, and God is merciful. How I wish I could express how this has changed me."

Chuck said: "Don't have to. I know God is so good. #Perspective. We take no day for granted."

I said: "I read your words to the football team. You just impacted 100 more, brother."

Chuck said: "Love you, brother."

The experience caused me to think back and remember all the children I've met who were fighting cancer. Many of them seemed to have an iron will. It is certainly one of the saddest and most tragic things in our world, but witnessing the strength and willingness to adapt within those little folks is a very special expression of mental toughness. The children you meet who have survived the battles seem to have a halo of enthusiasm. They will humble you.

Also in his book, David Brooks talks about suffering becoming a fearful gift, very different from that other gift we refer to as happiness. Suffering brings character. When you possess the level of mental toughness it requires to survive crucial events and ordeals that you encounter in life, you have the pleasure of knowing that no one can take that away from you. These are the things we remember most. All you have to do is listen to the things that athletes love to recall and talk about, and you will realize the value of ordeals.

The most significant reality that I've taken from the writings of Brooks is the fact that character is not just built through austerity and hardship; it is also built sweetly through love and pleasure. I have come to the realization that deep friendships with good people cause you to copy and absorb their traits.

The Athlete's Hierarchy of Needs

Some people who consider the implications of mental toughness reference Abraham Maslow. Maslow is responsible for what is referred to as a hierarchy of needs. I look at it as a system of viewing our lives as a climbing gauntlet of events required to ultimately become satisfied, autonomous and independent. This final condition at the top of what might be referred to as a pyramid is known as self actualization. In order to make it to this level, an individual must survive certain adversities and also satisfy specific needs. Surviving the adversities is a progression of demonstrating mental toughness through certain scenarios.

It's important to understand the process. Cornelius Plantinga was quoted has stated that "to try deliberately for self actualization is like trying very hard to fall asleep or to have a good time."

The lower needs must be met first. Most individuals, for example, don't achieve financial independence and security in a short period of time. Building for retirement is a process which requires sustained effort and a certain level of toughness to survive possible status changes in employment. Not everyone is capable of steady linear development. It is possible, for instance, that they never get to the stage of feeling socially secure. They struggle with finding a sense of belonging, which makes it very difficult for them to move into a mindset where they feel internally esteemed.

Personally, I feel that the process is long and hard in my profession. Coaching is highly dependent upon the performance of other individuals. You can be great at what you do, be committed at the highest level, have a tremendous work ethic and still lose an income. As a coach, you could get stuck in the quest for security and stability for a long period of time. I felt like I moved into the esteem phase fairly early in my career for the most part, but I could not move into becoming self actualized until I could realize financial security. I think coaches also need to have a steady demeanor and thick skin. I've experienced the top, the bottom, and everything in between. You must remain steady. Don't get too high and don't ever go low, no matter what is happening around you. It is important to think about remaining steady and focused toward the journey.

If we look specifically at the careers of the student athletes and consider the limited time we have to develop their performance as well as help them become productive citizens, we might consider applying this model to encompassing only the collegiate career. In this exercise, we can start from the bottom of the pyramid and identify the characteristics of self-actualized individuals as outlined by Maslow.

The first characteristic from the bottom up is extremely important and incredibly relevant — the athletes should have an accurate view of themselves and the world around them. This might seem simple, but often athletes who have NFL potential don't understand where they stand or the awesome commitment necessary to get where they want to go and stay there. Maslow talks about the disparity between the internal self and the external world. Mental toughness is important here because of the consistent level of production necessary as an athlete moves toward his senior season. They really need to understand the high standards they are being measured against. Remember that Vince Lombardi talked about mental toughness as "character in action." That is exactly what NFL scouts are looking for in a prospect.

The next characteristic is an earned sense of personal autonomy or freedom. Those on a team, however, must also conform to the rules of the organization. Athletes who are confident and mature are more likely to be more vocal. They recognize issues that need to be addressed, and they can also be extended a certain degree of trust during voluntary training periods.

The next characteristic is probably the most interesting. it is freshness of appreciation. After three or four years of grinding, they might only have a sense of freshness because they are happy to finally head to a new horizon. Maslow defines this characteristic as the individual seeing things with a new perspective and appreciating the breadth and wonder of things in the world. Realistically, if you experience success individually and as a team, you might be considered famous among your "nation." You get to travel all over the country and play on national television. You should feel very appreciative.

This flows right into the final characteristic — experiences that reflect significance, fulfillment and spirituality. These include joy, wonder, awe and ecstasy. Some call the college years the best of their lives. If they experienced these feelings throughout their college career, they might refer to themselves as an actualized athlete.

Most likely Maslow would not approve of my reduced model of his theory, but I believe that if you exhibit these characteristics, you have done well with your journey. You probably have felt a strong sense of belonging and esteem. The problem, sometimes, is that you will have to start at the bottom again upon graduating, and that is a tough reality. It could go all the way back to physiological needs not being satisfied because the training table is over, and you may not have an income. The outside world really doesn't care if you ran for a thousand yards or made All-Conference. The fact that you repeatedly demonstrated behavior characterized as what might be referred to as actualized is the most likely indicator of future success.

Persistence, resilience, confidence and discipline are associated with mental toughness, and the ingredients defining mental toughness are most certainly associated with self actualization. Abraham Maslow was quoted as stating, "If I were dropped out of a plane, into the ocean and told the nearest land was a thousand miles away, I'd still swim. And I'd despise the one who gave up." That sounds like mental toughness to me. In Maslow's model, not many individuals make it to the top of the pyramid.

Developing Mental Toughness

Anyone who studies mental toughness should be aware of James E. Loehr. Loehr has studied toughness as it is specifically applied to the athlete. The good news is that he believes that toughness is learned. Not only that, it can be learned at any stage in life. Loehr defines toughness as "the ability to consistently perform toward the upper range of your talent and skill regardless of competitive circumstances." That sums it up fairly well where competitive scenarios are concerned.

Strength and conditioning coaches are always searching for methods and ideas for developing toughness. That's one of the reasons that most collegiate football coaches would give for including a "winter conditioning" phase in their overall program. Football coaches invented "winter conditioning," and many individuals reference Bobby Bowden's "mat drills." Strength coaches were involved at the onset, but they are attempting to refine the process since there have been a number of unfortunate deaths that have occurred in winter conditioning through the years. Here are some other very simple points for consideration expressed by James Loehr:

No Discomfort—No Toughening

No Pushing—No Toughening

No Personal Confrontation—No Toughening

We currently have to view these very simple suggestions in a very calculated and careful manner. Is there a certain general or universal level of discomfort that we can prepare for? A tough heavy set of ten back squats isn't very comfortable. Conditioning can be very uncomfortable. Live practice drills in full pads can test your "collision tolerance." Practice and training tempo can give you a run for your money. You might feel like your team is tough enough and needs to focus on execution and become more skilled at what they specifically are asked to do on game day. You might have a big, strong team that you think plays the game soft. I've witnessed it. You might work with a group of coaches that simply fear separating themselves from tradition. They are going to do the same winter drills for the same number of days every year because it's "what they do."

I agree one hundred percent with Loehr's last point concerning personal confrontation. I have had some form of confrontation almost every day for thirty years. I look at it as strong coaching. You aren't looking to belittle anyone; you just want things done right. I don't think you get tougher unless you have a demanding coach always looking to see you go to the other level. We don't push people enough, and they need to be pushed more now than in the past. If we don't push them, we are cheating them out of the best opportunity to succeed.

I have always believed in emotion. Our high school coaches used to talk to us about taking and earning respect, because people from other school districts viewed us as coal miners and farmers. We were told they looked down on us. I'm not sure if they looked down on us or not, but the emotion that was generated by the idea of their disrespect was certainly a major motivator for us. Every one one of us wanted to knock somebody's lights out when we heard that we were disrespected. Football is a game of collision, and I just believe we hit harder, ran to the ball faster, tried to block you into the ground and fought you harder for four quarters when "emotion ran the show," and that is a quote from Loehr.

Loehr also states that the right type of emotions are empowering. He mentions energy, spirit, persistence, and confidence. Makes sense to me.

I like that fact that he also mentions the emotions that are disempowering, such as fatigue, fear, confusion and insecurity. If you feel tired, confused and insecure, you sure as hell will not execute.

Because I have been in the strength and conditioning business, my favorite aspect of the Loehr body of work is the belief that "in the final analysis, toughness is physical." He states that "thoughts and feelings are physical stuff too, they are just as real and every bit as fundamental to achievement as talent and skill." Most importantly, as related to conditioning, it is stated on page 20 of Loehr's book "The New Toughness Training for Sports" that, "A fundamental component of toughness is physical fitness." This tells us something that as coaches we already know very well—conditioning is a prerequisite to toughness.

The Gauntlet of Conditioning

Every football program in the United States has a somewhat different approach to conditioning. Personally, I don't feel that the type of conditioning required for football necessarily includes regimens even close to activities such as wrestling. If you merely consider energy systems and specificity, most individuals who possess a general level of fitness should be able to withstand football specific conditioning without throwing in the towel.

I do remember programs that incorporated the old Nautilus high tempo circuit to repeated bouts of failure, with garbage cans placed around the room to save the floor from vomit. I'm not sure how specific the training was to football, but you certainly developed a tolerance to discomfort. When we discovered that we might be sacrificing strength and power for tempo and toughness, the emphasis moved away from one set to failure. For those disciples of Arthur Jones and Dan Riley, it was a painful reality. Collegiate strength facilities now reflect a priority toward free form, closed chained barbell movement by the number of racks and platforms included in current designs. Penn State, for example, was a machine-oriented program for many years, and it is now equipped with 28 racks and platforms.

It is fairly obvious that United States military organizations believe that physical challenges not only develop mental toughness, but also are employed to weed out individuals who attempt to become members of higher level groups of warriors and decide they can't cut it. It seems like they feel that an individual must prove he or she is unusually mentally and physically tough to withstand being a member of an elite group.

It is interesting to see the nature of the specific challenges that a Navy Seal might have to endure. Hell Week, which is a very short training period in the total training of the Navy Seal, is designed with very specific training objectives in mind. It consists of five and a half days of continuous grueling activities designed to push the candidates to their absolute physical, mental and emotional limits—with only a total of four hours sleep throughout the entire evolution. The organization feels that the candidate will have to demonstrate that level of commitment just to merely successfully proceed with the training that follows.

Specific Navy Seal missions and tasks are described as follows.

1. "Walk nine miles over uneven terrain at night, carrying a 125-pound pack in 70-degree weather to objective; then retrace steps to extraction point. "

2. "Travel for five hours in an open rubber boat in 40-degree temperature and 30-foot swells; Beach the boat, cache/stage the equipment, and change from wet suit into dry clothes; then walk 16 miles during the next two nights over uneven terrain carrying an 80-pound pack, sleeping in two-hour increments, when possible, during a continuous rain."

3. "Travel for six hours in a zodiac in 0-degree temperature, then swim 600 meters in 36 degree water, crossing the surf zone to the beach; Change from wetsuit into winter gear and snow shoes, then walk 1.2 miles over uneven terrain and snow to objective; retrace steps to extraction point (24 hours total). "

There is no doubt, given these types of scenarios, that the individuals who sustain such assaults to mind and body are indeed special. The specificity of the demand must be achieved. Not only must it be achieved, the individuals must finish in a healthy state so that they remain active and productive to the organization. We might ask ourselves about cost effectiveness as we relate the concept to athletics, and more specifically football training and football practice. There is always a question about the need for "live drills in full pads." Personally, I feel live drills are vital; however, the recent precautions set forth to prevent concussions changes the entire perspective. it's a tough call.

When I coached with Steve Logan, he decided to start practice with the "Oklahoma drill" twice a week and also include other live drills such as angle tackle, stalk drill and chase drill. I am convinced that it made us a better football team. The types of training scenarios for a set of objectives specific to game day must be definitive and repetitive until perfectly executed.

If we are looking at the demands of collegiate football, there has been much written and much debated about what specific methods are most effective. There is a certain degree of common belief across the football world as well. I look at practice scripts, and they never really appear to be significantly different from coaching staff to coaching staff. You must be fundamentally sound, and each position group must rep its unique set of necessary skills.

Where Mental and Physical Toughness Meet

One of the first considerations you might consider as a coach is if you recruited toughness coming in the door. If you recruit talent and don't research character and toughness, it will most likely come back to bite you. Those players will inevitably work the system to their advantage.

If an athlete is talented but soft, he is not likely to be productive when physicality and durability are crucial, and that will be most of the time. Most people agree that assessing the characteristics of a collegiate prospect before a scholarship is offered is a good place to start. Thinking back to the purpose of "hell week" for the Navy Seals can raise consideration of a parallel that might be extended to the preparation of collegiate athletes. The purpose of "Hell Week" was stated as an experience which would reveal and establish the level of commitment needed to meet the incredible demands of a Navy Seal. This objective was not the least bit surprising to me.

For the entirety of my career, I have believed that conditioning is necessary to reinforce the team members with a relentless commitment and expose those who will shut it down. There will be those who believe that it is only necessary to train the specific energy systems relative to the game of football and avoid training scenarios that read into the danger zone. I would agree. We don't have to send our players into any Navy Seal missions anytime soon. Nevertheless, we also can't discount those laps around the field and grass drills that contributed to making Lombardi famous, or Bobby Bowden's "mat drills" that have been mimicked by so many coaches.

Mental toughness as expressed through physical performance is the essence of competition, and it is evident from the highest seat in the stadium. Excessive conditioning that is not relevant to the game is not going to hold up in a court of law. Excessive collision in practice sessions is going to be viewed as unnecessary, particularly because of what we now know about concussions. I don't fully buy into the belief that the tempo of practice alone prepares you for the ultimate challenge in a football game. I do believe that defensive pursuit drills, for example, can be amped up to the degree that they have a significant effect on football conditioning.

Anyone who coaches or leads men is going to rank mental toughness and physical toughness at the apex of the human dimension. It is key that this toughness is a team characteristic. A team that performs effectively and consistently in highly stressful situations with their backs against the wall is going to emerge as the victor because of fewer mental errors and penalties. When you play one of the military academies, for example, you quickly understand that if you don't match their machine-like efficiency in limiting mistakes, you can easily get beat. The recent success of the Naval Academy has been a great example to everyone in the football world. The mental toughness component is clearly apparent, even when they are playing the top programs in the country.

The experts will continue to study and attempt to define toughness. Many believe that it can be developed. We can definitely state at this point that it has been and will always continue to be a vital component of collegiate football. Mental and physical toughness are the premium fuel for overachievement.

2nd Platoon 1st Force Reconnaissance Company, USMC cold and wet, Fort Lewis, Washington 1997.

"The more you sweat in peace the less you bleed in war."

By John Dailey

I was the platoon sergeant for a force reconnaissance platoon, enjoying a beer in a pub in Darwin, Australia, late in the evening of September 11, 2001. Of course, with the time difference, it was just a little after 8 am on the East Coast. The soccer game on TV suddenly switched to images of the twin towers smoking. We finished our beers and headed back to the ship, knowing nothing was ever going to be the same and that it wouldn't be long before we were involved.

We found ourselves in Afghanistan two months later and spent the next few months conducting long-range vehicle patrols in the desert lowlands south of Kandahar—driving all night, setting up ambushes on roadways, looking for the Taliban, sometimes finding them. It was freezing cold, and we hadn't expected to be here when we left the states.

Between driving all night and keeping security during the day, we were lucky if we managed three to four hours of sleep. Food was Meals Ready to Eat (MRE's,) usually eaten cold. Through it all, one thought was never far from my mind: Our training had prepared us for this because it had been harder than this. We had been more tired, colder and hungrier than this before.

As platoon sergeant it was my job to push them in training, just like my platoon sergeants had done. I remember a training exercise in the winter in the mountains of Fort Lewis, Washington. After a weeklong patrol across rugged terrain, we were finally moving to our extraction point. We had no food left. We were filling our canteens with snow and relying on body heat to melt it so we could drink. We moved to a spot in the trees at the edge of the clearing where the helicopter was scheduled to pick us up. We all kept each other awake listening to the static of the radio, waiting for the voice of the pilot and the slap of rotor blades through the trees.

Instead we received a call: extract has moved. The new coordinates were at least a day away—over a mountain. At the time I wanted to scream or throw something. We all wanted to, but we didn't. We packed up, picked up, and crossed the mountain. I would think back to that mission and others like it years later in Afghanistan and Iraq, and every time I did it made me smile. We had put ourselves through worse, so that this would not break us.

CHAPTER THREE

LOYALTY AND FEROCITY

"Whatever thy put thy hand to, do it with all thy might." –*Ecclesiastes 9:10*

God didn't mince words with this scripture. You need to live your life at a full-speed tempo. Ferocity might be a strong word, but if you want to accomplish anything that people remember, you need to wake up every day with your hair on fire. Football is just an incredibly wonderful method of expressing the influence of the surging level of testosterone that drives young men to seek competition. There are not many experiences in a young man's life that measure up to catching a winning touchdown pass, making a big hit on a kickoff, sacking a quarterback or one of the other many game-day scenarios where you can establish a name for yourself on national television. There are a number of potential rewards that collegiate football players have available to them in the realm of exposure that currently exists within today's media.

There is much talk about the way things have changed over the past few decades concerning the decline of physical activity among today's youth. I started playing organized football in Western Pennsylvania around third or fourth grade. In Washington, Pennsylvania there was an organized league of grade school teams that played at a miniature field and stadium named the Bronson House. You learned very early what it meant to compete, and some strong rivalries developed, even at the grade school level. It wasn't uncommon to end up in a physical conflict with some other grade school student if you were playing Bronson House football and ventured into a neighborhood of one of the opposing schools. Even at that age, the competitive feelings were intense.

Back then, no one came home until dark when school wasn't in session. In the summer, we got up early and collected a large group of friends before noon. We wasted no time choosing teams and organizing some type of competitive activity. We played football on the back roads in the neighborhoods that were light in traffic. We found baseball diamonds that were temporarily abandoned. We played tackle football if we could locate a grass field that resembled a rectangle. We played basketball anywhere that we could find a hoop, even if it was in the driveway of a stranger. We wrestled in the grass, simply because people in Pennsylvania will wrestle just about anywhere.

Life Lessons

When I think back, I recognize that the tempo and spirit of my competitive life began very early. We had fun every day because we were competing at some level. You knew the kids in the neighborhood who were the most athletic and you knew the kids who might not have been equally blessed, but everyone would compete. We respected each other and developed great friendships. I can't remember anyone who wasn't tough. Even if you picked somebody last, they never felt bad, because we all cared about each other. I feel proud when I think about that. It would be difficult to imagine how many times we jumped, sprinted or changed direction throughout the course of a day. There were times when we rotated four different sports activities before the sun went down.

There was never a means of direct communication with your parents. They had to hunt you down, and that was the way we liked it. I can't remember anyone getting into a whole lot of mischief back then besides becoming immersed in a game and being late for dinner. I broke my foot one day and limped home for twelve blocks, which wasn't very smart. I broke my arm in two places playing tackle football in three inches of snow and got in trouble because I had promised my mother I was not going to play football. I remember that I was embarrassed because we looked at each other as weak if someone said they were hurt. My ulna was sticking through my skin, so I had no choice in the matter.

My father was a very successful high school coach, and he would bring me along to practices when I was a young boy. I learned two words shortly after learning my parent's names. The first word was "hit," and the second word was "hustle." The word "hustle" took on a very deep meaning, and it came to encompass multiple interpretations. It might refer to the way you move from drill to drill, the way the defense pursues the ball, a full speed trap block or simply the way a team takes the practice field coming through the gate. The word "hit" means you are playing the game with a high level of physicality. You were going to stick your face in somebody's numbers with violence. If you saw stars, that was probably good. You got your "bell rung," but you would be OK. It's kind of like when a boxer takes a good punch but doesn't go down.

I can distinctly remember the times when I saw stars in high school and college. You don't forget those plays, even though you might have forgot where you were for a moment at the time. Of course, we know now that it is not a good thing. Whatever the case, my dad's team were known to outhustle and outhit people, and that went a long way. He still says, "Football is fun. Fun if you win and win if you hit." So true. When you talk about ferocity, his teams had that quality. The defense was flying to the ball, and the offense highlighted crushing trap blocks. It was eleven people dedicated to doing their jobs full speed on every single repetition.

You can think back on those times and then look at where you are in life and really appreciate those two simple words. I'm proud that they became part of my personality. I go to bed every night thinking about how early I can get up and make something happen the next day. I feel like I can get in a half day's work while the rest of the world is sleeping. I've always felt that it was really easy to outwork people because they barely make it in the door on time and they are always thinking about the next break. They never learned to hustle.

I had an experience in high school that was somewhat shocking to me involving the relationship with labor and management. I have always been proud of the coal and steel industry. My mother worked for a steel company and helped me get summer jobs in the steel mill every year during the summer. The mill paid good money, and I worked in several divisions of the plant. One summer they placed me in a division referred to as "electric furnace," which sounded frightening and hot as hell.

My first night we started working at a fever pitch pace, and I made certain that I stayed very alert. I was working on the midnight shift. We were rolling hard with what felt like a purpose, and it made me feel like I was at a football practice. I got into a rhythm, and even though I was assigned some type of basic chore, I was in hustle mode. Time went by quickly, and before long it was 2 a.m. and time for a break. Everyone moved around and got comfortable on some chairs and benches, and someone started to turn some lights out. I got very confused and asked some guy what was going on. He explained to me that the night's quota was met, and that these men were unionized. Since they achieved the quota in two hours, they were finished for the night and going to sleep. I was shocked that we were now expected to sleep for six hours and go home. It made me feel sick. I started to realize that the atrocities that management had committed toward labor over the years were now being reciprocated. I asked to be moved shortly after that. The fact that people were getting paid to sleep just didn't resonate with me.

I will say that the other divisions of the plant were not like that. For example, I had been assigned most of the time as a "big flattener" helper.

We would hook giant slabs of hot titanium to an overhead crane and guide them into a huge flattening machine. It was not a situation where you could afford mistakes. If you didn't hustle, you could be seriously injured. I know that unions can provide safety and insure that workers get pensions when they retire. That summer, I became aware of the abuses on both sides of the coin. Eventually the plant was bought out by another company. I'm not sure of all the reasons, but I always return to the scripture, Ecclesiastes 9:10, that started this chapter.

Let's further explore the powerful meaning behind that little three letter word "hit." Hit refers to being in attack mode and not being afraid to sacrifice your body. It is a mentality. You are willing to be the first man to attack a wedge on a kickoff. In life, you have few reservations, and you are never intimidated. You seek out a way to overachieve, and you have plan of action to accomplish lofty goals with high expectations.

In high school we had a whole category of drills that focused on full speed live collisions. They had catchy names like the "Meat Grinder," "Bucket of Blood," and "Bull in the Ring." Learning to block and tackle with more violence and physicality certainty molds you into a more effective football player, but it also provides you with an aggressive mentality. If that mentality becomes part of the culture, you have a much better chance of success as a football program. Any success in my life can probably be traced back to those two words: "hustle" and "hit."

Somewhere in my childhood is the point in my life where I started to connect the concept of allegiance or loyalty with ferocity. I use that word because passion is just not a strong enough expression. In Western Pennsylvania, football was indeed a microcosm of life, and it was also a reflection of the immigrant experience. Whether you were greatly talented or you had limited athletic ability, people respected your work ethic and commitment. If you survived summer camp in my high school program, you had achieved membership, and membership never came easy. The word "passion" might describe the way you felt about your community, the people within the community and of course, your teammates. You wanted to live up the expectations of the tradition. Blue collar expectations don't always result in a guaranteed victory, but a defeat might be forgiven if you have represented the hardcore, never-quit, play-with-pain mentality of the culture. A lack of toughness would never be forgiven. The two words, "hustle" and "hit," would not be compromised. I witnessed the power of collective ferocity. I witnessed the installation of a shared sense of integrity within individuals that would, somewhere down the line, be recognized as having a lifelong impact.

Uncompromised Loyalty

This early experience provided me with a special appreciation for the United States military. I've always believed that they just do things the right way and that the parallels with a football program are undeniable. The level of required loyalty is non-negotiable and necessary to success. Of course the ferocity of war is a different type of fury, but the attitude and mentality have to be almost the same.

When you believe these things and you accept a coaching position, it is almost impossible to compromise what you have ingrained in your soul. And when someone suggests that you must change your standard ever so slightly, you are a torn individual. The very thought almost makes you physically ill. If a Marine Corps general asked a Marine Corps drill instructor to overlook a disheveled bunk because of that particular Marine's giftedness to hit a target at 500 yards, how would that drill instructor respond? If you asked a strength coach to overlook an athlete who came into a workout five minutes late because of his ability to catch a football, how should he respond? Should he resign on the spot because of his unwavering belief in accountability? Should he be reduced to a lesser standard because of his desire to keep feeding his family?

How many individuals in our profession have frequently been subjected to this type of scenario? I would submit that in 2018 this is a frequent occurrence. It is a sickening thought. The reason it is sickening is because it throws good men into internal struggle. I've been there more times than I want to admit, and I have been forced to find innovative methods of redemption. You have to outsmart the situation. That might be the true measure of the ability to survive in this profession—to maintain self respect and honor within a sometimes unprincipled environment. It is simply the age-old issue of talent versus compliance and the team or organization being bigger than the individual. The Marines talk about being part of something bigger than yourself. Gray areas always make things cloudy for everybody. The point here is that military organizations have no gray areas, and individuals who possess a ferocity associated with loyalty are wired the same way.

Coaches who view the world this way, coaches like me, are likely to experience an inner struggle that borders upon torture throughout their career. The nature of the profession is to put your time into a program serving a certain set of colors, and when the time is right or when you get fired, go find another set of colors to serve. If you look at the typical resume of a collegiate coach, it usually includes a long list of experiences with short terms of employment at each institution. Of course, when things go south, you need to move on and find a paycheck. Inevitably, every year you will encounter programs with losing records. Those programs make changes, and thus goes the merry-go-round.

When I accepted the job at East Carolina University in 1991, I learned very quickly that ECU had parallels with the culture where I was raised. Even the people I met were similar to people I had known and respected through my life. You can call it "blue collar," "down to earth," "carrying a chip," or whatever other descriptive fits—it is a community that has a ferocious sense of loyalty. It felt like home. A lot of people I knew growing up never wanted to leave home. Many had never been very far from Western Pennsylvania. I think my dad was in his fifties when he stepped on a plane for the first time. Leaving your extended family is really tough when you spent every Sunday of your young life at Grandma's house.

It was just never natural to me to be looking around for another job and a new set of colors when I viewed it as if I joined the Army or Navy or Marines or Air Force and it would be a lifetime connection. If I were a Marine, I would want "Semper fi " written in my coffin because of the way I feel about loyalty. I honestly don't believe that I would have lived a very long life in the military because my sense of loyalty would have most likely placed me into very dangerous situations.

During my first ten years at East Carolina, our head coach Steve Logan would explain to me at that no matter who you were, a fan base would simply tire of your presence—or possibly your eccentricities. You would be forced to move on, and it really didn't matter how you felt. I would get aggravated when he would tell me that, because I felt like he was establishing some self-fulfilling prophecy. That kind of conversation was never good for me. It caused me to involved myself in hedonistic activities like sitting on a bar stool for half a day. I could never accept the fact that I would have to sacrifice my sense of loyalty because some knucklehead couldn't make a tackle.

I cried like a little kid who lost his mother at the mall on my way to Chapel Hill to start my coaching experience at Carolina. I cried as if I had been court martialed like that Marine in "A Few Good Men." I was confused. I kept telling myself how normal this was in my profession, that I was simply helping my family. That was bullshit. The reality was that I had poured my soul into those colors, and I just wasn't your typical coach who welcomed change—even with a significant raise in salary. I needed another bar stool to sit on for a while. We defeated ECU 24-21 that season, and I had to leave the field early. I gave everything I had to UNC that year, just like any other year, but I couldn't go hug a bunch of heartbroken kids that I cared about so much. It was the strangest feeling ever. I'd say it probably took five years off my life.

Somewhere around year four, I started to feel halfway comfortable in my new colors and maybe not so much like Benedict Arnold, who I despise by the way. The Tar Heels would play the Pirates five more times—with one loss that came during Butch Davis' first year at UNC.

Over time, you learn to become a convert. You have little choice in the matter; it's collegiate football. I have been back at East Carolina now for almost eight years, and I have worn those original colors again for four more meetings with UNC. George Washington would have gladly hung Benedict Arnold if he could have gotten his hands on him. But hey, they say, 'This ain't the military and it's just a sport.' Really?

Understanding the Human Will

I think back sometimes on the Pittsburgh Steelers of the seventies. I think about Chuck Noll, Terry Bradshaw, Franco Harris, Lynn Swann, Mean Joe Greene, Rocky Blier, LT Greenwood, Jack Ham, Roy Gerela, Mel Blount, Jack Lambert, Andy Russell, Dwight White, John Stallworth, Mike Wagner and more. They were a family with culture. The roster didn't change a whole lot. You wonder how much the continuity contributed to their great success. Things are much different now. It seems like a lot of players are rented out for short periods of time, then they move on to new colors—just like a lot of coaches.

Our objective is to investigate the human dimension, or the human will. Remember that the human will is the "chief incalculable." If I am a player in today's world of collegiate football, I see coaches getting paid big money. I might have to get used to a new position coach every year, because so many of them are trying to move up the ladder. If I'm in a program in the AAC I'm losing my head coach and his staff, because as soon as he sees success, he's moving to the Power 5 conference to become a millionaire. Should a player think that he could keep his coaches by not winning too many games? How crazy is that thought? Maybe a ferocity linked to loyalty is just a Utopian notion. I know that I am going to keep coaching that way, because its in my DNA. I'm proud to say that I am entering my eighteenth year in one place. I prefer to be about tradition. It's always a battle, it will always be a battle, and it is not going to get easier. You just have to embrace the grind and sell the program. You have to be smart. You are a guru of charismatic rapport. Keep teaching a warrior ethos, and find a way.

As a strength and conditioning coach you are always searching for buzz words or phrases. I love the words relentless and fanatical, and they are used frequently by coaches. We all try to live by those words, but they have not been good for my sleeping habits. You are always thinking about what you might do the next day. If you want to be competitive, there is no other way to live. Most strength and conditioning coaches wake up at 4:30 a.m., because they always have a 6 a.m. group. It might be 6 a.m., but your athletes will follow your lead. Because of that, you need to be relentless in your preparation for the next day. You have to sit down and think about what just happened with each athlete that day and try to continuously make it better.

University of North Carolina Tar Heels 2001

Very proud to have been part of John Bunting's staff with a cast of "rock star" coaches.

The expectation must be very high. It is very difficult to be associated with individuals who can't appreciate incredible opportunities. They must be reminded every day. Sometimes an athlete has to be reminded to continue to trust the process. There are no guarantees that you will be a starter or win a championship, but the commitment level must always be there, whatever the situation. You must train in a fanatical manner so that you have the best opportunity to win and the best opportunity to sign an NFL contract. No one should be comfortable with regret, and if you don't make every day count, it will come back to haunt you somewhere along the way.

The "tempo" of training previously mentioned in the preceding chapter was characterized by the words "high intensity." Those words referred to training to failure with limited rest. Offensive schemes in today's realm of collegiate football employ a "tempo" concept. Players quickly get lined up for the next play with the objective of preventing the defense from effectively substituting multiple packages and also causing fatigue in the opposition. The Marine Corps War Fighting Skills Manual states that "tempo is a weapon." The parallels between the concepts employed in warfare and football are interestingly similar. First you must establish a furious tempo, which is athletically equated with effort and conditioning. Next you have what is referred to as maneuver warfare, which would be your game plan. You would construct this plan after many hours of studying the opposition.

The objective of extreme tempo and a high level of physicality is to cause attrition. Of course, victory doesn't result from attrition alone; it will be the result of both attrition and maneuver. Next we toss in the element of surprise. In football we have trick plays, but the most effective element of surprise would be the adjustments made during the game. Sometimes they might be readjustments. The best coaches have already installed a system that facilitates an arsenal of adjustments that can be relied upon on game day. The Marines refer this threefold combined arsenal—attrition, maneuver and surprise—as combat power.

The Importance of Speed and Focus

These concepts continue to deepen as we study the process. There are two concepts that act as a subset to combat power—speed and focus. Now the parallels seem to be even more pronounced. We can learn a lot from the Marine Corps by simply studying and applying the concepts. Not only are the implications toward the preparation of the game itself, but also for off-season training. The War Fighting Manual states that speed over time is tempo, and that speed is also a weapon in itself. It also states that relative speed is more significant than absolute speed. If we look at running speed as possibly the primary component and most important characteristic of a football team, then we must prioritize accordingly. That indicates that we must train the component that is referred to as absolute speed. This is the superior speed that seizes the initiative.

We know from watching the game over many years that putting a few burners in key skilled positions is going to produce very effective weaponry (provided that they can play the game of football). Relative speed would be referred to as repeated sprint ability. If I have a few players who are moving at a sub 4.40 pace forty times over three hours, there will most likely be an impact. Conditioning a team to operate at a high level of repeated sprint ability is a no brainer. You will need to remember to recruit speed. I like the formula of character plus skills plus speed when building a football team. If the priority order of those three ingredients gets confused, however, it will be problematic for your team.

It is also stated in the manual that speed is a prerequisite to maneuver and surprise, which brings us back to tempo. The evolution of offensive football has arrived at what is currently a fever pitch tempo. That indicates that the preparation requires a very specific type of conditioning. Generally speaking, football coaches have never liked activities that are slow moving. It is in their nature to want to see that "hustle." If you ask coaches to come into the weight room and stand around while your group recovers between sets, they will appear to be tortured.

When I coached at UNC, the head coach assigned five young assistants to the weight room to observe and conduct position-specific movement drills at the appropriate time. Those men lasted one week. The were mesmerized that we coached the same thing four times for two-hour segments every single day. That is eight hours of steady coaching. They were cross-eyed in three days. Because I coached football for many years and experienced the tempo of collegiate practices myself back in the seventies, I get this.

The way that the Marine Corps defines focus is "the convergence of effects in time and space on an objective." In the game of football, penalties, turnovers and mental mistakes are expressions of a lack of focus. These factors diminish combat power. Anytime you talk about the list of variables that impact the outcome of a football game, they can almost always be attributed to some type of mental lapse. Tempo comes into play here as well, because fatigue contributes significantly to mental error. A team or unit that is poorly conditioned will be vulnerable both physically and mentally as the game progresses. One mistake committed late in a close game can be the difference in the outcome.

I conducted my own study on this phenomenon during one of our off-seasons. I had athletes run for a certain number of intervals at 9 mph to place them in a state of fatigue. I think I referred to it as a twelve-play drive (30 seconds on and 30 seconds off). At the end of the twelve minutes, I kept them on the treadmill at 7.5 mph. As they continued to run, I gave them simple flashcard equations similar to what we experienced in grade school. They had five seconds to answer. There were many variables to consider. First, we assumed everyone could answer simple equations, under normal circumstances in five seconds. These were very simple in the initial test such as 4x4 = __ or 24-9 = ___. As we progressed to additional sessions creating the same exact level of pre-fatigue, we increased the difficulty level of the questions. We wanted to see how deeply they could focus. As each level increased in difficulty, we switched from a time limit to the total time it took them to answer. Of course, we also recorded correct answers.

As expected, the level of fatigue contributed to errors. It was difficult to account for baseline intelligence, but the nature of the question probably did not surpass an eighth grade level. As the level of the test increased in difficulty, we began to consider questions related to football scenarios, and possibly game week scenarios. Unfortunately, my bright ideas began to surpass the budget. We couldn't quite take it to the next level, but I still believe it is great food for thought, especially with the current advancements in technology. I would envision a set of virtual goggles that would include game tape and questions about the upcoming opponent, and the athlete would have to answer very specific questions in a state of fatigue. The questions would be specific to each position. This method would have a positive impact on understanding the power of the human dimension.

Knowing Your Opponent

I went to college as a quarterback but moved to strong corner on defense. I was quick and had very good feet, but I was not as fast as some of the opposing receivers. Because I grew up with football in my life, I knew the power of film study. I saw it as an equalizer because people don't change what they believe is working for them, and they also develop habits that tip you off. I'm quite sure the Marines study the enemy. I look at it as another level of personal preparation. You might see a slight inside alignment of a receiver that would tip an outside pattern or a change in the stance of an offensive tackle that would indicate a pass play. Certain teams might be highly predictable related to down and distance.

We already know the amount of time that coaches spend in studying an opponent. The real question is, how much time does the athlete invest in studying the opponent? That would be above and beyond position meetings. Those study habits are another factor that raises the human dimension meter. We should also mention here that there are coaches, and then there are deliberate coaches. These are the coaches that desire to raise the human element by investing extra time into each individual. This is challenging for coaches, because they spend a great amount of time in the office in season, and then they are away somewhere recruiting for extended periods as well. The NCAA has provided another two hours a week during the summer when they can study film with players or work on position specifics. The coaches that take advantage of that time will gain an edge. The important key here is that they are gaining an edge with the human potential, because they are grooming mental cues and knowledge of the game as well as the finer points of coordination. Knowledge that gives you a step or a quicker reaction time can be vital. Perfection to detail is power.

As an athlete, your commitment to a ferocious sense of loyalty should be evident in your daily preparation. The concept of tempo should be at the forefront. Coaches will need to create that type of environment within the athletic setting, whether it be through the essence of the training program, the nature of practice sessions, or preferably both. The most effective way to create a vibrant tempo in your program is through the heart of each individual player. It is interesting that the Marines describe war as a social phenomenon. The attitude and chemistry within a collegiate football team make it an interactive phenomenon as well.

The War Fighting Skills Manual specifically states that, "the essential dynamic of a social phenomenon such as war is competitive human interaction, rather than the dynamic of art and science." I find that statement to be incredibly powerful and interestingly profound. The quality of human interaction on a football team is vital, and it is directly related to winning. The time and effort you invest into nurturing productive relationships pay dividends, especially during tough times. Success and failure will always begin with the level of character of each individual.

The War Fighting Manual goes on to state that, "It is because of this dynamic of human interaction that fortitude, perseverance, boldness, esprit, and other traits not explainable by art or science are so essential in war. It is the power of the human will that ultimately influence a war because it is a dynamic process of human competition." I can't think of anything more beautifully expressed that directly parallels a football team. We already know from a previous chapter that there is a term referred to as friction which can take on many forms. Friction is eliminated by effective forms of human interaction, and the possession and operation of those favorable traits promote effective forms of future interaction.

The term "dynamic" is a powerful word that applies very well toward what is intended to be conveyed in this chapter. The Marine Corps, as well as other military organizations, place tremendous emphasis on traits that become common among every member. We should emphasize here that it is mandatory that they become common. One of those traits, appropriate to the theme of this chapter, is initiative. Initiative refers to having the confidence and drive to get something started. It's about standing up when something needs to happen or calling someone out when things are not right. NFL scouts are always going to ask me if a young man is vocal. Rising seniors are expected to have leadership qualities. These type of questions usually receive a shallow response.

The People You Want In Your Foxhole

An athlete can possess character and to some extent be vocal, but in my opinion, you only make it to the NFL with ferocity. It is the individual who only knows this one gear in everything he does who provides himself with that type of opportunity. Of course he is vocal, because he can't understand why anyone around him would lack the same commitment. The people with this type of personality have the type of initiative that establishes traditions. They have to find methods of expressing their passion before their head explodes.

I've seen my share of these individuals over the years, including the man who raised me. My father was a competitive wild man. If he wasn't coaching, he was playing in some high level softball league. If the weather was bad, he was playing dart ball or possibly an Italian game where you throw fingers and call out a number. That game somehow inevitably resulted in conflict, because the players were intensely competitive. I can recognize these ferocious individuals within a couple of days, or maybe in the first hour that we begin to train them. They are the people you want in your foxhole.

I coached a linebacker at ECU who I mention often when I refer to these type of individuals; his name is Jeff Kerr. He was like a heat-seeking missile on the field. He was about initiative every single day. He is deservedly memorable. He was extremely demanding of his teammates, and he became en enforcer for developing all of the characteristics that coaches want to see in a successful football team. Of course, it always helps when a player has a physical presence. Jeff came into the program at 190 pounds and worked his way up to 240 . As his stature improved, he became more confident as a team leader, but he was always "out in front" of the training since the day he stepped in the door. His teammates fully expected him to assume the initiative, simply because of the identity that he projected. Athletes who take the initiative seem to be automatically successful beyond their collegiate careers. Persistence is very powerful. Loyalty is the engine that drives initiative.

The most important times for those who lead a life of ferocity are times of deep adversity. This is how we further identify those individuals who simply persist and never retreat. Through my coaching experience, I have observed many different types of adversity both within individuals and within a team. Whether an athlete has experienced a childhood of fortune or fatherlessness, they all seem to require a high level of guidance and rejuvenated spirit following a poor season. You can't allow any inkling of negativity to permeate the environment. I don't like to think or admit that the current generation is not as fiercely competitive as those of two decades ago, but I do believe that they have too many avenues of escape. I am always fearful of the decline of football. I see more individuals who seem to avoid competitive situations and acquire afflictions such as headaches, backaches and possibly a pulled muscle. I'm hoping this is just my imagination, and I realize that I am always seeking out individuals who seem to have excuses, but I may have become ultra sensitive to crushing softness and falsehood. I might need a good counselor. Sometimes I refer to scripture.

Hebrews 10:36 states that, "You need to persevere so that when you have done the will of God, you will receive what he has promised." To me, a big part of doing the will of God, provided you believe in scripture of course, is relentless pursuit of your potential. We are all aware of the countless examples of incredible perseverance through the many decades and even centuries of competitive achievement. Right now we are talking about ferocity in the game of football—people like Dick Butkus, Ronnie Lott, Ray Nitschke, Jack Lambert, and many others.

I might be biased because I played defensive back, but to me there is no one that represented ferocity as well as Jack Tatum. I encourage defensive backs to watch Tatum's highlights and take a lesson from those who played the game in a manner where they were feared. Football is still a hardcore, violent game that gives back to its participants if it is played in that manner. Tatum even had a poem revised to honor his style of play which I especially love, because it talks about pirates.

It is entitled "The Autumn Wind":

The autumn wind is a pirate
blustering in from sea.
With a rollicking song,
he sweeps along,
swaggering voicelessly.
His face is weather beaten,
he wears a hooded sash
with silver hat about his head,
and a bristling black mustache.
He growls as he storms the country,
a villain big and bold
and the trees all shake,
and quiver and quake,
as he robs them of their gold.

The autumn wind is a raider
pillaging just for fun.
He'll knock you round and
upside down and laugh when
he's conquered and won.

Tatum was viewed by many as a ruthless individual who played the game the way it was meant to be played. He stated once that, "My idea of a good hit is when the victim wakes up with train whistles in his head." He was also nicknamed "The Assassin." Tatum had critics, particularly after one of his hits ended up with a receiver being paralyzed for life. This style would be outlawed if he played within today's rules. Tatum came into the NFL with a chip on his shoulder because several NFL teams determined him to be too small to be drafted, and he made a name for himself with his sense of physicality and became a three-time Pro Bowler.

I see Tatum as a man who lived his athletic life with loyalty and ferocity. He was highly regarded at Ohio State University, where he established a name for himself. He was a dedicated and proud Buckeye who would come back and speak to the team on occasion. Athletically he was naturally explosive, but small in stature for a safety. He obviously built a fire within his heart and took it to his game. When people start inserting your name into poems reflecting on how you played the game of football and that poem is recited on NFL Films Network, you will be remembered. When Tatum stated that he was "paid to be a warhead" he meant it in the literal sense. He played with a ferocious, intimidating and memorable style of play.

Randy's Way

A not-so-famous example of the highly motivating effect of loyalty is a situation that I personally witnessed over a 25-year period. My wife and I bought a little beach house around 1996 in Emerald Isle, North Carolina. It is my favorite town in the USA. The location is not far from

Camp Lejeune, the well known Marine Corps base. One day I was standing on my porch and across the street I saw a man sitting in a wheelchair with a dark suntan and a young girl in a bikini who appeared to be taking care of him. It didn't take long to find out who he was or learn his story. Major Randy Hebert was in the Gulf War as an engineer, and he had developed ALS. We met his incredible wife Kim and his two small children Kyle and Nicole. I describe Kim as incredible, because she has never appeared to waiver in her undying support for her husband and family. She went so far as to enlist Congressman Walter B Jones to convince the VA to increase the type of nursing care that Randy requires and deserves. At that time, Randy was given two to five years to live.

We are talking about military traits in this chapter. We are talking about a ferocious sense of loyalty, which was physically expressed in the game of football by Jack Tatum and others like him. A whole different example of ferocious loyalty is exhibited by a man who has not been able to move or speak. This is what we might refer to as the power of an undaunted heart and a mind dedicated to his wife and children. Major Randy Hebert still lives on in 2018. I recently spoke to him about contributing some anecdotal experiences to this publication. He responded back to me by blinking his eyes. Those who take care of him go through the alphabet, and he blinks when the letter that he chooses is verbalized. It is a tedious process.

Here is an excerpt from a letter Randy wrote several years ago: "I would like to think my longevity is a direct result of the fact that I am a Marine—motivated and mentally tough. But the reality is, God made me a Marine for a reason, and only by the grace of God have I lived this long. I received the grace because of my personal relationship with God. With my relationship, I also have received a true peace that surpasses human understanding. My purpose, duty and obligation is first to God, to glorify Him, and second to my wife and children, to support them. My hope is that by continuing to persevere that I will glorify God and be an example of God's power and love for my family. When you look at me and see my smile, I hope it's obvious the Spirit of God lives in me."

There is a book being written about Randy, and friends constructed a wheelchair runway to the beach because he loves the outdoors. Both are named "Randy's Way." Randy was known for his ability to run long distances and smoke every other Marine through the finish. I can only imagine how many days he envisioned himself running down the beach fifty yards in front of these amateurs getting in their morning jog. I don't think I can really find the words to express the level of loyalty that Randy has expressed toward his family. You just believe what you see, and you keep shaking your head in amazement. You go back to the Marine Corps War Fighting Skills Manual, and I think that whenever the new edition comes out, his story must be included. Twenty-five years later Randy is still persevering, and he is now enjoying his two children as young adults. He's been there for his children through times when they had the opportunity to make him proud. They are no doubt better human beings by the mere fact their father was present and watching. Enough said. Semper Fi.

I've heard athletes and friends say to each other, "You're my dog." I'm not sure they understand the full implication. This speech shows us that being like a dog is something we truly should aspire to.

A Tribute to the Dog
The Ultimate Speech on Loyalty

Senator George Graham Vest

"The best friend a man has in the world may turn against him and become his enemy. His son or daughter that he has reared with loving care may prove ungrateful. Those who area nearest and dearest to us, those whom we trust with our happiness and our good nam,e may become traitors to their faith. The money that a man has he may lose. A man's reputation may be sacrificed in a moment of ill-considered action. The people who are prone to fall on their knees to do us honor when success is with us may be the first to throw the stone of malice when failure settles its cloud upon our heads.

The one absolutely unselfish friend that man can have in this selfish world, the one that never deserts him, the one that never proves ungrateful or treacherous, is his dog. A man's dog stands by him in prosperity and in poverty, in health and sickness. He will sleep on the cold ground, where the wintry winds blow and the snow drives fiercely, if only he may be near his master's side. He will kiss the hand that has no food to offer; he will lick the wounds and sores that come in counter with the roughness of the world. He guards the sleep of his pauper master as if he were a prince, when all friend's dessert, he remains. When riches take wings, and reputation falls to pieces, he is a constant in his love as the sun in its journey through the heavens. If fortune drives the master forth an outcast in the world, friendless and homeless, the faithful dog asks no higher privilege than that of accompanying him, to guard him against danger, to fight against his enemies, and when the last scene of all comes, and death takes his master in its embrace and his body is laid away in the cold ground, no matter if all other friends pursue their way, there by the graveside will the noble dog be found, his head between his paws, his eyes sad, but open with alert watchfulness, faithful and true even in death. "

People have been slaughtering each other for centuries. Loyalty is not common, it is instead very difficult to sustain in any human organization. Humans are greedy and sinful, not to mention envious. We might take a lesson from the dog with regard to true loyalty. That is very sad to think about; but if we as coaches stand on the table for loyalty and convey to these young people that we don't have to go through life with reluctance toward the fact that loyalty is meaningful, we can hopefully make a difference. God never waivers in his message as to how we should treat each other.

3rd Platoon 1st Force Reconnaissance Company, USMC conducting desert operations 1996.

"Loyalty is a cohesive force that forges individuals into a team."
– Coach John Wooden

By John Dailey

In Marine Corps special operations, one of the primary missions we train for is 'direct action.' These missions usually involve arriving at a bad guy's house in the middle of the night, moving silently to maintain the element of surprise, then blowing the door off its hinges and flooding the building with shooters as quickly as possible.

Once surprise is lost, we rely on speed and violence of action to catch the targets off-guard before they can mount a resistance. In order to execute a direct-action raid successfully, thousands of hours are put into practice for what might take no more than a minute to complete. To operate at the highest levels takes incredible amounts of training and skill, but in a nutshell success boils down to every man focusing on two key ideas: lone shooters and danger areas.

Is there a teammate alone? if so, go to him to protect him and fight with him.

Is there a danger area, anywhere we could be shot at from? If so, cover it. We put ourselves between the threat and the team and know without looking that everyone else is doing the same. We can't look to see if it's happening. If we don't know our teammates are covering us we can't execute with the singlemindedness that ensures success.

Once in Iraq we were going after a high value target, a former regime intelligence officer who was now a key leader in the insurgency. That night my team was driving—we took turns as lead assault, secondary assault, external security, and vehicles. The primary assault team moved to the door. The team's breacher, Andy, placed the explosive charge on the door. The assistant breacher noticed a propane cylinder sitting by the door and moved it—better safe than sorry, but this prevented him from holding the charge as Andy stretched out the firing tube. No one is exactly sure how, but the blasting caps came out of the charge and the tension of the firing tube snapped them back. They stuck to Andy's vest, under his arm. A team member saw movement inside the house so the team quickly pulled into position.

Andy set off the charge. The point man moved to the door which was still there, and Andy fell to the ground, injured by the charge. The assault continued, and the team stepped over him like they had practiced a thousand times. This was not a lack of loyalty, but rather an example of it. They knew we would get to him. The last man, a medic, dropped a tourniquet on his chest and told him, "Get that on your arm," because the assault team knew that those of us outside on security would take care of him. They also knew that a pause in the assault would cause a loss of momentum and stall the initiative the explosive breach provided, leaving the rest of the team vulnerable.

CHAPTER FOUR
THE PROCESS OF DEVELOPING SELF DISCIPLINE

It is somewhere around 1995, and I'm pulling into the parking lot of the training facility at East Carolina University at 3 a.m. I'm getting ready to meet three members of the football team who were absent from yesterday's workout. They were contacted and instructed to meet me at the gate to the practice fields at 3:30 a.m. As I preface this experience, let me provide a few facts about why I think the way I think. This will require me to recall my own personal collegiate experience. I was no angel in college; I stayed out late on weekends, drank, missed some classes and got into a fight in the cafeteria. Some things I choose not to mention, but in my own defense I will state that many of these behaviors were more easily accepted as a common norm back then, and some were even applauded. I'm not proud of those hard-learned experiences, but I certainly did learn.

Where football was concerned, I never missed a practice, never gave less than 100 percent effort during training or practice and never missed a workout. I never missed a game and I was never, ever late for anything. In fact, I went to the stadium five hours before every home game just to focus on what I needed to do. I played with concussions and broken bones. I competed every day because I was afraid of losing my job, and

I would have rather been burned at the stake than miss any game reps. I wanted to be in the game for every play on defense and special teams. I hated to make any kind of mental error on the field. I really just wanted

to play a perfect game relative to alignment, assignment, and responsibility. I recently saw an article that an old teammate found and posted on Facebook from 1979, stating that I was a hard hitter. That put a smile on my face, even almost forty years later. I had to work hard to be good, and I've always been proud of that. I remember my teammates as a group of exceptionally tough

Helping my good friend Jim Fleming chart pass patterns. Currently the Head Coach for the Rhode Island Rams.

young men, and those memories influence your standards as a coach.

It has always been almost impossible for me to understand how any individual who receives a college scholarship at the highest level could refuse to pour every ounce of his soul into that commitment. I think most individuals in a fan base feel that way as well, but unfortunately not every member of a collegiate football team has the sense of allegiance and level of self-discipline that one might hope for. I don't know how many times I've witnessed incidences of behavior considered to be shameful to a program, but it is certainly in the hundreds. Many occurrences are kept "on the low," mostly because coaches don't want the individuals they sold so hard through the recruiting process to prove them wrong. It is hard to accept, and it is an embarrassment. If a young man must be suspended for any period of time, the program is without a player in that position, and depth in college football is crucial to success.

It's 3:30 a.m. that morning at the training facility, and no one is showing up. I round up my assistant coaches, and we head to "Scott Hall" where the players reside. We know where the individuals are located, so we go straight to their doors and knock loudly and identify ourselves. I was having a flashback to serving warrants during my time as a police officer in south Florida. We were getting no answer, so we banged louder and individuals throughout the dorm started to wake up. One player opens his door with the words, "Sorry coach, my alarm didn't go off". Typical excuse. It ranks up there with flat tires and deaths of multiple grandmothers. Still no answer at the other door. I'm not going to admit that we forced the door open. My memory somewhat escapes me. I think it was stuck and we offered assistance.

We were dressed and on the field by 4:10 a.m. Time for edification. We started with several gassers to get warmed up, followed by ten Vietnams. In Vietnams, you run the length of the field with up- downs every five yards. Next were some push-ups, up-downs, rocket jumps and burpees in sets of twenty-five repetitions. This is a great sequence of exercises, followed by bear crawls, and they completed five or six rounds. Next, we farmers-walked heavy dumbbells for fifty yards and combined that activity with pencil rolls. Pencil rolls have a tendency to make you dizzy. The finale was a bear crawl through the front gate as the first group of the day arrived so they could witness what they would not ever want to be a part of. It also rained for the entire session that particular day, so the offenders were quite muddy.

Conditioning is Discipline

Any strength and conditioning coach over the age of fifty who has worked at the collegiate level no doubt has memories of these type of experiences. It was expected to be part of the job; you were the "discipline guy." It was discussed in the job interview. I had a player named Jerry Dillon who described me in the newspaper as a criminal. You were proud of your name-brand brutal sequence of events to deter inappropriate behavior and violations of team rules. If you didn't have a system of dealing with these issues, football coaches would think you were soft, and most likely you would not be around very long.

I had a defensive lineman who couldn't lose weight one year, and his coach thought he could be good if he could just make a commitment to fitness and conditioning. I drove him about five miles out of town, dropped him off in the parking lot of some cowboy bar, and instructed him to jog back to the facility. I had to park several times so he could stay ahead. I should have packed a lunch for myself. He made it back unscathed. He has been coaching for many years now, and every time he sees me he reminds me of that incident. You would think it was the proudest accomplishment of his life. I'm glad it was memorable, but the point was that I was willing to go to any extent to help him get it done. He got it done at his pace, but he got it done.

There is an aerobic device that we use called a stepmill. It can be a great teacher. It is undefeated. Usually an athlete would complete a certain number of floors at a certain pace, but the problem came when the individual was tempted to stop and step down when fatigue set in. I had an answer for that. I use a whole roll of athletic tape for each forearm and taped the individual to the rails to help him stay on the device. Nobody was injured, and we didn't force the athletes to go beyond what a normal human being could handle. The point was made, and another memorable punitive procedure was put in the books for people to exaggerate.

I believe one hundred percent, and I've stated many times, that conditioning is discipline. It is the only vehicle of awareness that induces fear and anxiety. The team members understand that there are natural consequences in life, and the consequences for poor decisions involve discomfort. Of course, we know that discipline has a much deeper meaning than just running the hell out of someone. I coached with a seasoned ball coach named Rick Smith, and I like what he would always say about conditioning: "Conditioning precedes mental toughness."

Well, amen and halleluiah. You can't think about being tough if you are not in shape. If anything in this narrative will be repeated time and time again, it is that fatigue will trump toughness every time. This is a very simple concept, and it is always and forever true.

The quickest and longest lasting response to a sequence of disciplinary wonders was exhibited by twin brothers named Daren and David Hart. The twins did not make it to their lifting group on time early in their freshmen year. They ended up in the doghouse, which is very uncharacteristic for them. These young men only knew one speed, and they never gave a thought to trying to cheat the punishment. In fact, they attacked it and made it their friend. In other words, they were more than happy to kick their own asses if they thought they may get tougher. They elevated their levels of self-discipline, didn't change the tempo for even a second, and refused to show pain.

The Hart twins completed five rounds of six activities with no rest and a total of 750 repetitions. That is an experience I will always remember as a coach; they were not going to be broken and did not blink. They made no excuses and offered no complaints. They had me thinking I would have to devise something tougher to make an impact. I was more than a little surprised. When I saw them the next day, I had to tell them that they had crushed the punishment to the point of causing me to question it. Their response was that it was the hardest thing they had ever done, and that there would be no way that they would put themselves in a situation to experience it again. You could have fooled me. It was no surprise that they became great players and even greater vocal leaders.

One year, coach Steve Logan got totally fed up with players missing classes. He chose the old punish-the-whole-team concept to pressure the offenders. We met at 5:30 a.m. at the track and did a smorgasbord of 800s, 400s and 200s for an hour. We did this for about two weeks in a row. One morning we ran twenty-eight 110's. We changed it up to keep it fresh. Some of our players thought this might go for a whole semester. When they were finally informed that they didn't have to get up and run, you would have thought they had hit the lottery. There was a new commitment to accountability. This was, of course, a testimony to the power of peer pressure—one of the oldest tricks in the book. There will always be those who argue for the welfare of those who committed no wrongs, but the truth is that sometimes it takes extreme pressures to produce extreme results.

Truth and Consequences

We've all heard stories of the punitive measures toward individuals in military organizations who might violate "codes" of discipline. Much of this is Hollywood depiction, but the concept of discipline is certainly vital to every military organization. The process of learning to do things effectively and without human error requires teaching and nurturing, and of course relentless repetition depending on the task. If we take a journey back into the history books, we can discover that is a well-established fact that British soldiers were sentenced to dozens of lashes for violating military discipline. Some might say that is the reason they lost , but I'm convinced, from what I've read, that George Washington also had a short-term tolerance level for lack of discipline.

I've read several accounts of consequences, such as standing in a freezing river as the result of not making it to a specific destination within a specific time limit, as part of the training to be accepted into one of the highest-regarded elite military organizations. I brought an individual from one of those organizations to speak to our football team one year and he talked about being "professionally prepared for timing and circumstance." That kind of said it all.

There were several summers throughout my career when we ran the dreaded 300s around the field on Tuesdays. These were very tough because of the required times and the short rest intervals. I think most of the team went to bed early on Monday nights, and I know that they started thinking about those runs at least 24 hours in advance. We had two linemen on our team who were good players and fun to be around. They were inseparable throughout their career. Their names were Ronnie Suddith and Jamie Gray. Every Tuesday they could be seen sitting at their lockers two hours before their group time, just staring at the floor and occasionally verbalizing. They looked serious. This was their weekly routine, just to prepare themselves to run the 300s.

It became known to the whole team, and in one sense it was comical to look in and know where they would be sitting every week. On the other hand, they were learning a great lesson in self-discipline. I say that because they never failed. It was tough to weigh 300 pounds and make seven 300s with a 30-second rest. You had to train all summer to get to that point. The purpose was toughness and self-discipline. That's it. You started with two reps with a minute rest, and you progressed from there. I loved the fact that they thought about it for a whole day. It was truly "game day" every Tuesday.

The Supremacy of Self-Discipline

On a more civilized note, the word discipline is derived from the word disciplinaire, which does not refer to some form of extreme discomfort but rather instruction. I always tell players that we want men coaching men. Say it: "Coach me, coach". Can we think about using the word "collaborative," or does it always need to be corrective at some level? You often hear, when an athlete seems to elevate his level of self-discipline in collegiate football, that he is "taking the coaching." I've thought of devising a scale that starts with low corrective status at the bottom and finishes at the top with the highest form of collaboration. Honestly, I don't feel that collaboration is possible to a great extent in the realm of collegiate football; however, I have seen many highly mature young men that love to play and learn the game.

I believe that the level of self-discipline a young man brings through the door is directly related to the environment that he has experienced in the home. I also believe that even with the best environment, every young athlete coming through the door is going to need to stay on the rise of developing his personal level of self-discipline. That is the only way athletes can expect to maximize their potential during the short period of time they have to compete.

College is a vast learning experience, which is why it is referred to as higher learning. What might not be realized, especially for the collegiate athlete, is the depth of learning that takes place outside the classroom. Realistically, a collegiate football player can have a major within an academic discipline, but he will also be required to unofficially minor in strength and conditioning and consider football knowledge as a second major. The self-discipline level required to excel in all three areas is extremely demanding, and it goes back to value of deliberate coaching. Deliberate coaching would indicate that a highly prepared coach can make a significant impact in the success of an athlete simply because of his ability to teach.

I view performance enhancement as a separate discipline – athletes have an opportunity to learn through practical experience. Hopefully, they appreciate and recognize the results experienced through an organized and methodical plan to improve specific physical attributes. They must develop technical expertise in executing a wide variety of patterns involving overload. They learn methods and progressions of preventing soft tissue and joint injuries. They enhance sport-specific movement patterns through improving postural integrity and strengthening specific muscle groups. They learn strategies of enhancing mobility and thereby becoming more fluid.

The extreme self-discipline of a deliberate coach can be burdensome. About ten years ago I started to get extremely frustrated with the range of issues that I had been confronted with in this business for the previous two decades — issues with accountability, attitude, drug abuse, discipline, poor spirit, apathy, attrition, coaching changes and more. I made moves to leave the coaching world to take a job training Special Ops Marines. I heard that the only thing you had a problem with in that realm was preventing individuals from injuring themselves from working too hard, so it sounded like a winner to me.

The bottom line was that I was offered a much better deal to remain in collegiate athletics. God reeled me back in and made my calling in life very clear to me, even though I didn't want it. I was fed up with feeling like a glorified social worker. Sure, I had coached a ton of great young men, and I had witnessed many who changed significantly for the better. You always say to yourself that even if you changed one life, it was worth it. The problem is, sometimes you kick the hell out of yourself and your own family in the process. You see the struggles of your own children and wonder if things would have been better if you were home more. But time and again you go back and embrace the opportunity, especially when you are having a great day with some problem child and the glitter returns to your veins. You have a spiritual reckoning with yourself and some kind of revelation of your deep hidden love for humankind.

I had a talk with our team last week about my objective for the current training phase. It was very specific. I said, "Coach C wants to encourage you to raise your level of self-discipline. It happens one of two ways—collaborative or corrective. You can either learn by encountering a man coaching men or by my foot in your tail. Because it has been revealed to me as my calling, I am willing to die for it. I'm not going to get to heaven unless I give you self-discipline; that's how serious it is. God told me to love you unconditionally and do my job." This calling has been clearly communicated to me from above, so I'm assuming that when He wants me to do something else it will be just as clear.

When you explain self-discipline to young people, it is imperative to understand that the pounding that you impose on some wild child is only going to go so far. At some point, they will have to internalize the characteristic of discipline and hold themselves to the fire. I can sit here and recall multiple strategies and innovative progressions of physical pain that will spin your head around, but the problem is that once an individual hits about age twenty, the learning curve is fairly stiff. I think it is important that they understand the benefit to those around them— as well as to themselves—in order to affect a change. Self-discipline is equated with winning. I have to remind them that they can help their teammates win. When a group of young men collectively decide to adopt a high level of self-discipline, there will be power in their hard work and in their agreement.

Developing a Habit of Excellence

Another way we can view discipline is through the simple repetition of activity. In other words, we don't necessarily provide individuals the opportunity to think a lot about what we have them doing. They are developing a habit—grooving a motor learning pattern through perfectly performing an activity on demand. Habits govern performance, and ultimately habits govern our lives. Discipline is considered by some to be blind—not necessarily right or wrong. It can be expressed physically, but we develop repetitive ways of thinking as well. You can discipline yourself toward both positive and negative behavior.

I always think about my golf swing. I get a bucket of balls and go to the range. If I make a mistake, but know how to make a correction and return to an effective swing, I continue to practice. If I continue to slice or hook with no correction, I'm going home. Someone else can finish hitting those balls. I would be grooving a bad swing and encouraging a poor motor learning pattern. If we are going to practice, we must practice effectively. A good coach does not allow poor execution of a skill without correction, whatever the activity. Understanding discipline is important both to the coach and the athlete from the standpoint of perfection of execution. This may be best demonstrated within the realm of martial arts. In that discipline, the objective is to relentlessly practice movement until it becomes an automatic response.

If you think about discipline of behavior having a developmental effect on habit, it is quite easy to see the reason for attention to detail and an intolerance for anything less than perfection. If we consider mistakes in practice that are never corrected, as well as the tolerance toward something like bad body language, we can quickly understand how these factors can lead to failure. We understand that everyone is practicing discipline and forming personal habits. On a team, ultimately the overall habits will dictate morale. It all starts with who we are disciplining ourselves to become.

I don't think coaches give enough deep thought to this process. When you take over a football program, you have an opportunity to immediately decide and demonstrate how things will be done "your way". You will have the opportunity to interview, educate, and observe what you have inherited in relation to athletes and coaches. Some coaches have already decided to bring their own staff because they are familiar with the expectation and the process that accompanies that expectation. Some have already made the decision that there will not be an inch of compromise as related to the required level of discipline, because they recognize discipline as the process whereby habits are formed.

Personally, I believe that if you have any other mindset, you will be short-lived. Once the expectation is delivered, it must be adhered to with absolutely no deviation from the plan. There can be no weakness. Every athlete must be treated the same and measured against the same standards of performance. All the demands must be enforced with no hesitation. That includes all athletic, academic, and social responsibilities. It sounds like a rigid way to live, and it's a lot of work, but I've seen so many athletes disappear from the program over the years that I see no other avenues.

Repetition to Reach Perfection

Since we are referring to military virtues and the military model, we should probably consider the basic premise that is at the heart of military training known as "boot camp." This is where individuals learn to do the very smallest of things to perfection over and over again. They must learn to execute perfectly on demand. Perfect execution on demand is the objective of every offensive coordinator. How many times should we run a play before we feel that it will be perfectly executed? When a coach considers all of the various scenarios and potential adjustments that an offense has to be prepared to execute, it becomes apparent that repetition and meetings are crucial just to run one play successfully. After all, these young athletes are the same age as military recruits. The mistakes that they make during a game are not life and death, but they can get a coach fired in a hurry.

Sometimes we find it necessary to revert back to Lombardi on these issues, especially when it comes to the most basic of football principles. Coach Lombardi said, "You teach discipline by doing something over and over, by repetition and rote, especially in a game like football when you have very little time to decide what you're going to do, so what you do is react almost instinctively, naturally. You have done it so many times, over and over and over again." Lombardi was referring to what it takes to develop effective habits. He believed that habits were formed from beliefs, and that beliefs were established out of "self –talk." It's a belief that you can get the job done and consider yourself a winner because you possess the necessary qualities to do so. However, these qualities are not instilled without a price tag.

The Marines talk about the "crucible" of entry-level training—about "steel being tempered to withstand the stresses of future challenges even more severe and testing" as they begin to lay the foundation on the day they report. When we train collegiate football players, we must build them from the inside out, and we must begin with an ethos just like that in military organizations. The most challenging objective for today's collegiate football player is what the Marine Corps seems to value right at the top of the list of its most valued cornerstones—that Marines should "subordinate their own self-interest to the overall interest of the group." This is an incredibly important quality to instill in today's athlete. Today's athlete, remember, is a member of the narcissistic, entitled millennial generation, so it is particularly challenging for them to put the team ahead of themselves.

It is precisely because of this that I believe that you must begin with the enhancement of the qualities of the individual. The student-athletes may be self-absorbed, but they are also hopefully educated to a level whereby they can comprehend the power of a strong personal foundation. As individuals, they need to be turned on to the type of deliberate coaching that reinforces the acquisition of attributes that awaken the highest level of self-esteem. They must develop an iron will within themselves, and that development starts within the heart of the mind. I will always go back to the fact that the majority of the recruits coming through the door are standing on sand. Building something always begins with a foundation. I also believe that each habit that Lombardi referred to—courage, sacrifice, passion, commitment, hard work, discipline and mental toughness—needs its own foundation.

Building Lives

We know that Jesus Christ was a carpenter. There must be incredible honor in the art of building if our Savior chose it as a profession. In His Sermon on the Mount in Matthew 7, He talks about a foundation of either rock or sand. We know that we need to build on the rock. We also know that He was referring to lives, not skyscrapers. Everyone must build a life. We as coaches need to pursue a system of development that builds our athletes from the inside out. An attractive house that can't withstand the pressure of high wind will be destroyed. I've seen recruits that enter the program and have the appearance of strength and toughness. Within a week's time, as they engage in your program, you expose their physical weaknesses day by day, and often they show a low mental toughness threshold as well.

These are athletes that have experienced success at the high school level on sheer talent alone; they have often neglected strength training and have experienced minimal challenges to mental toughness. The seven habits that Lombardi mentions are seldom in place at the highest level. Any one of the seven that is exposed as being weak is going to be a hindrance. The individual has not built a solid foundation, and the level of Division I competition is at a totally different level. The speed of the game and the intensity of collision is going to be like a Category 5 hurricane blowing through a house built on sand. Sometimes a structure that looks ideal from the outside arrives at a tragic ending. We must identify these individuals early, strengthen their minds, and provide them with foundational strength physically and mentally so that they can quickly adapt to the elevated demand.

Lombardi cited discipline as one of the seven necessary habits to success. The quote we are all familiar with is, "I've never known a successful man who, deep down in his heart, did not appreciate the discipline it takes to win. There is something in great men that needs discipline, that really yearns for and needs head-to-head combat." Obviously, the key words here are "successful man" and "great men." The individual must have the desire to be great. He must have the desire to seek "head to head combat."

Lombardi had so many amazing insights that have lifelong universal application. You almost have to think that sometimes that God was speaking through this man. He believed that hard work was discipline, in and of itself. I believe that conditioning is, in and of itself, a vehicle that establishes and maintains discipline. That's why I've maintained that the toughness factor of what you do always outweighs the scientific, energy system rationale—as long as it is safe. There probably wasn't anyone on Lombardi's staff thinking about rhabdomyolysis when they were administering those famous grass drills. Somehow they survived it all.

Lombardi also wrote that "discipline helps you embrace and endure the pain associated with change." Whatever challenge gets thrown your way, you are better prepared to handle it simply because you've learned self-control. Most coaches could write a dissertation on this topic based upon their own experiences in this profession. All you have to do is read the staff bios, and you discover that the sum of schools where the football staff has previously coached is a bit mind boggling. Coaches and their families have to maintain self-control through discipline just to survive as a unit. Many times, it's the family, more than the coach, that is forced to endure the pain of change. As long as we are finding parallels with the military, these situations are still much easier than not knowing if someone is coming home at all.

Military personnel have to find a way to prepare their families for incredible stress even as they are leading soldiers through stressful situations on the field of battle.

Jocko Willink is known for his thoughts on taking ownership as well as writing the bestseller *Discipline Equals Freedom*. The message of the former Navy Seal is in line with the thoughts of Lombardi regarding the responsibility of those in leadership roles. In fact, I would have to think that Jocko must have read some of the statements and thoughts of the Lombardi belief system at one time or another. There are a few different ways that you might equate discipline with freedom, but I don't think it was ever said more eloquently or more accurately than the way that Vince Lombardi Jr. described it in his book. "The freedom comes from having a core set of values and possessing the discipline, courage and sense of duty and obedience to those values, so that when we are challenged, we respond almost unconsciously in ways that are in accordance with our values."

Crucial Values for Athletes

The values that we hope to instill in collegiate football players are no secret, and there is a powerful consensus about the ones that should be considered essential. They are hammered and re-hammered through various approaches and responsibilities in leadership roles. If you've been around long enough, it becomes both interesting and somewhat entertaining to observe the tactical plan of the next coach in line. Not a whole lot needs to be added to the list of Lombardi's seven habits. In fact, many of them are themes for the chapters in this book. The Marines have narrowed it down to discipline and spirit. These are mentioned in the initial speech to those who are beginning the boot camp training process. Those two principles are probably enough to think about and embrace as you begin your journey through the grind.

I believe that a huge factor in this quest for discipline is the ability for a collegiate athlete to manage his or her day. Football players are usually miserable with this task. They are required to get out of bed, make it to their workout time, eat, go to class, report to study hall, get treatment in the training room, show up for their appointment with their tutor, eat again, meet with their position group, practice, eat again, study, and most important to them, charge their cell phone and get a few tweets out before turning in.

Time management is one of the most glaring challenges for the collegiate athlete. Never before have they had to fit so many activities into one single day and arrive on time. Over the years I have been witness to hundreds of individuals who just do not believe it is necessary to be on time. It is such a hard lesson. It is interesting to note that very seldom will we see an individual arrive late for practice. They are on display to the entire organization. I've only worked for one coach over the years where this was a frequent occurrence that evidently was allowable. You get what you demand.

I believe that it would be significantly worthwhile to have every athlete take a time management seminar coming in the door. It is certainly a key step in the quest for a high level of self-discipline. I can't help but refer back to another Lombardi quote: "I believe a man should be on time—not a minute late, not 10 seconds late—but on time for things. I believe that a man who is late for meetings or for the bus won't run his pass routes right. He will be sloppy." Here we go back to the importance of the small things in a program.

If you want to have a successful football program, you must start with how you want to run your practice and exactly how you want your coaches to coach. That is one of the things that I was most impressed with during my four years as the strength coach for Butch Davis at UNC. He knew exactly what he wanted from every minute of practice, and he had some level of control over all three phases. I'm not sure every coach was elated with that at times, but I enjoyed the fact that he was obsessed with the details of a practice. Through Super Bowl victories and national championships, Butch incorporated this into his approach. This should be no surprise to anyone who understands Lombardi's quote. To me, it's like basic math. You can't get to calculus without it. There must be attention to detail in everything you hope to convey.

From a training and strength and conditioning perspective, there is nothing more vital to improved performance than self-discipline. We know that training results are cumulative. We know that an individual can become "detrained" in a very brief period of time. The NCAA is most likely to continue to reduce mandatory training time for the collegiate athlete, and it wouldn't surprise me if spring football was eliminated. If a team doesn't qualify for a bowl game, that team goes home as soon as the players complete final exams. There is no mandatory strength training or extra practices. The players are on their own for six weeks. If they discontinue training, they of course, lose the training effect. They lose lean mass, gain body fat, lose explosive power, become slower and possibly lose range of motion as well.

If they are self-disciplined and follow the program you provide for them, they should continue to build on what you envisioned for them in their progressive development. A collegiate football player must also possess position-specific skills. The process of sharpening and maintaining those skills must not be compromised. Here is where we call to light another analogy from military organizations in that soldiers develop a higher skill in specific areas after they graduate from basic training. They must continue to train and improve those skills to be effective. A combat medic has life and death skills; he or she cannot afford six weeks of inactivity. Athletes come to college to receive an education, so there is no question that choosing a field of study and relentlessly working to capture their dream within that field should be their primary focus every day. As an athlete, to be able to accomplish that mission and excel on the field of competition is a major challenge. This challenge is going to dictate who they become when they step through the gateway to the big world out there.

Athletes have at least nine weeks each year which are referred to as discretionary. This is where self-discipline must continue to kick in. Continuous education on the effects of detraining must be present, and a structured program must continue as well. I've seen dozens of athletes undulate throughout their career toward understanding consistency in training all aspects of performance. Not only do athletes not understand the impact of detraining, they are happy to take advantage of any free time made available because they feel overwhelmed by their daily demands. Military organizations indoctrinate self-discipline at the highest level as a way of life. The closer we can get to that, the better chance we will have to put a team on the field at an optimum level.

Another factor that needs to be addressed is providing guidance toward turning in assignments and papers on time, as well as the vital importance of steady successful achievement throughout a grading period. When athletes save everything until the end and scramble to finish papers at the conclusion of a grading period, the last thing on their mind is to voluntarily complete a training session. Nothing matters if you are not eligible. An abandonment of academic responsibilities can be a vicious cycle—ending with no degree in hand because of a total abandonment during the senior in-season semester. It's just another situation where self-discipline makes a huge difference in the end result of a highly demanding process.

As a coach, you are going to have to make a decision on how far you are willing to go and maybe how insanely adamant you appear to be in establishing self-discipline within your football team. The animated extremists are my personal favorites. I don't think you have to scream and appear to be deranged. You just need to act immediately—every day and every time—when something even remotely smells like undisciplined behavior.

Achieving Like-mindedness

When a team has finally established a common sense of self-discipline, it also develops like-mindedness and unity of purpose. When the team has collectively arrived at this point, all of the resources of each individual, each position group, each unit and the team as a whole will be optimized. Everything begins to develop with machine-like precision. The heart is right.

I've been through a number of football seasons through my thirty-plus years career when it was glaringly evident that individuals were conflicted with divided mindsets. This can be deadly on game day. It sometimes occurs within organizations that are in a state of transition. This transition process can be anywhere from smooth to troublesome, but it usually has challenges until the coach brings in his "own people." Even individuals who know nothing of the game of football can recognize an organization that is conflicted. There are a hundred individuals who participate one way or another, and it is important to narrow the focus of the objective so that we can have one mind. Millennials and the Z generation have been said to respond to mission statements and mantras, and they really can make a difference. Some mission statements that I like include:

"Be the change"

"One team, one fight, one fight, one family"

"Game day, every day, every day, game day"

"Embrace the grind"

"Love to run, love to hit"

"Can't nobody do what we do"

"Smart, fast together"

One of the best examples of teamwork in our society is that of the surgical team. Of course, this team could be said to be analogous with a military special operations unit. We are not talking about an extremely large number of individuals here. In fact, we are referring to a small number of individuals who are very highly trained as individuals but also understand that the team must be a priority because they operate in life-or-death situations.

I view football as somewhat of a life-or-death situation because of the probable death of a coach's career without the vital commitment of all those within his realm of supervision. He is responsible for teaching and motivating the entire organization to operate with one mind. He must communicate that daily to everyone within the organization. In my opinion, it is crucial that he personally interacts with anyone who is significant within the organization. Delegation should be minimal. I'm just one of those folks who believes strongly in loyalty, and if you give me a slight pat on the back I'm going to go to war for you on that much higher of a level. All you have to do is let me know. I like it in the trenches.

The surgical team consists of the physicians, the nurses and the anesthesiologist. As soon as the blood starts to flow, the members of the team take on the same level of importance. No mistakes can be afforded if the team expects to be successful. Mistakes can take a life in an instant. Mistakes on the football field have enormous impact because of the nature of the game. Defensive players have territorial responsibilities. If you are confused with "gap responsibility," you can expect to experience defeat. If you "blow a coverage," the opposition easily puts points on the board. Offensively, you are programmed to read a situation in a moment and adjust on a dime. If the left tackle fails on a given pass protection, the quarterback could be eliminated for the entire playing season.

Developing like-mindedness through a heightened level of self-discipline first requires every team member to speak the same way about the team. Some examples of statements they should all make:

"We must be full speed every rep"

"Everyone must pass the conditioning test"

"We must all take personal responsibility and correct mistakes"

"We must take on the characteristics of a brotherhood"

"We must avoid off-the-field issues"

"We must share the same commitment to the off-season program"

"We must study the game"

"We must be coachable"

"We must learn to play with pain"

Every player must think the same way about themselves, all those around them and the team as a whole. As soon as any negative talk begins to occur, it becomes contagious like a disease. There are those individuals out there known as "locker room lawyers" who commonly only think about themselves and are happy to cause turmoil under duress. They have no self-discipline.

Developing the quality of self-discipline within a football team is invaluable. If strength and conditioning coaches can understand what it takes to accomplish this on a daily basis, they should continue to get paid accordingly.

Marine Corps Special Operations Command Detachment -1, pre-deployment training in Nevada, 2003.

"Now if you are going to win any battle you have to do one thing. You have to make the mind run the body. Never let the body tell the mind what to do. The body will always give up. It is always tired in the morning, noon, and night. But the body is never tired if the mind is not tired."

- Gen George S. Patton

By John Dailey

In my opinion, after over twenty years of service in the Marines, most of that with Special Operations, there is nothing more valuable or more misunderstood than self-discipline. Willpower is the civilian variant of self-discipline, and most believe it's a magical quality that only certain people possess: "Oh, I would love to get in shape, or lose weight, or learn to play the guitar, but I just don't have the willpower."

Willpower, or self-discipline, is no different than a muscle; you develop it by using it. This is an area where the Marine Corps shines, because we build discipline by putting you in situations that suck. The first stage of developing self-discipline is the recognition that things that suck don't kill you. As Nietzsche said they "make you stronger."

102

This was a lesson I learned repeatedly, but will never forget thanks to our Marine Combatant Dive School. We were trained to maintain equanimity, to get through situations using our head when it was possible and unrelenting violence when it was not. The ability to remain calm was instilled through stress inoculation, built into all of our training. At dive school, it began with sharking. Once trained in the basics of SCUBA we'd swim, in a two-man team, in endless circles along the bottom of the twenty-foot deep pool, waiting. Rule number one was never leave your buddy. Rule number two was never lose your air tanks. It comes without warning—two instructors attack, rip your mouthpiece out, turn off the air, pull your mask away and toss it—chlorine burns your eyes and forces its way up your nose. They take your weight belt, fins and scatter them across the bottom of the pool. Then they tie your air hose and turn the air back on to pressurize it—it stiffens the hose, tightening the knots. Now they grab your tanks, pull at the straps, try to tear them away as you tumble across the bottom. You're screwed if you let them, so you hold on to the straps, curl up in a ball, take your beating, hold on to your breath and wait for it to stop.

Finally, it does–this is the crucial time. You choke back panic. White sparkles appear at the corners of your eyes. You know these come first, soon your vision will begin to tunnel, the blackness collapsing from the periphery inward until you black out, but you resist the urge to bolt for the surface. You can see it, the light above, but that would be failure. You focus on the problem and do the counterintuitive: turn your air off, put the tangled mouthpiece in your mouth and expel the little air remaining in your burning lungs to clear it. You suck in water and get a half breath from the knotted hose. That releases the pressure. Now you can work to untie the knots, your chest is heaving. Once the knots are free you can turn the air back on; now you can breathe. Then you can figure out what you need to do: find your mask, put it on, tilt your head back and press the top of the mask tight against your forehead, exhale through your nose to clear the water out, find your fins, put them on, your weight belt, and get your tank straps back around your shoulders. It sucks bad, but each time you're more confident in your ability to save yourself.

Each time you miss a meal, or carry a heavy load, or sleep on rocky ground, or don't sleep at all, it becomes easier to do it again. When you have hardened yourself with adversity it becomes easier to get up at 5 a.m. for the gym, or go out for a run when there is snow on the ground, because that is what you do. When those things become easier, everything else does too. The development of self-discipline is fostered by forced discipline, but it doesn't truly become an individual action until you take it upon yourself.

Self-discipline picks up when motivation fades and allows those who have developed it to be in charge of their own destiny, not the voice in their heads that says, "Let's wait until later, or tomorrow, or next week to do what needs to be done. That's why it's important to develop it and keep it sharp by doing things you don't want to do and don't have to do.

CHAPTER FIVE
THE UNIQUE ESSENCE OF LEADERSHIP ON THE COLLEGIATE GRIDIRON

There have been countless books written about leadership. The word is thrown around like cheap grass seed; you see it and hear it everywhere. Some appoint themselves experts and don't appear to have ever led anybody. There are leadership academies and leadership seminars. You can pay people big money to teach you how to lead. When NFL scouts ask me if our rising seniors have leadership qualities, I always want to ask, "in accordance with whose standards"? I honestly have known very few collegiate athletes that I would classify as true leaders under the standards that I feel are necessary for effective influence of one's peers. Many of the best athletes that you coach who possess talent and physical stature are great people, but they allow others to so influence their thinking that they are more interested in their own personal path to success than the responsibility associated with true leadership. They are thinking about how they look on game tape, how they plan to stay healthy, or who they might end up choosing as their agent. They might even have people around them who are already thinking about how they can get a piece of their signing bonus. Sometimes it can be a heavy burden to carry.

I believe that a player must first and foremost have a strong charismatic quality, bordering on intimidation, to have any chance of being classified as a leader within a collegiate football program. Yes, you must be a "badass." Should you be physically intimidating? Not necessarily, but it doesn't hurt if you are 6'5", 320 and you play the game and train with a nasty demeanor. You will have a chance to influence your teammates. If you make plays, play hard every snap, and have a ferocious

Waiting to lead the team out with one of the most admirable human beings I ever met; Steve Logan.

passion for the game along with an impressive stature, you have another leadership feather in your cap. If we add the characteristic of having the same expectation of your teammates that you have of yourself—if they might feel that you would possibly grab them by the neck—that's also meaningful. Many years ago, if you were winning bar fights on the weekends, it was a strong indicator that you might be a leader. That kind of experience is no longer necessary. Losing a scholarship will not help you lead.

I had the pleasure of coaching Julius Peppers during his off season as a rising senior at North Carolina. The reason I mention Julius is that the attention he received from ten different directions every day was amazing, and possibly sometimes burdensome. Julius had a fairly quiet demeanor and he worked extremely hard, even with the level of skill, size and power that he was blessed with. I had him at a 4.55 forty-yard dash at 285 lbs., and we ended that season with an 8-5 record and a Peach Bowl victory over Auburn. Some of the losses we experienced were unnecessary. For example, we blew a 24-point lead over Wake Forest.

I can't remember any time when Peppers became irate or got in anybody's face, but you had to consider that he had a new head coach heading into his senior year and he was about to become a millionaire. He had to stay healthy to keep his value. Julius was probably not overcome with a responsibility to lead. He was a great player, a great teammate and would become a tremendous representative of his university. Could he have been a factor in winning any of those five games that we lost, if he was just a straight-up confrontational ass kicker? Maybe.

As a coach, you never forget the individuals you coached who were genuine leaders. They make your job easy. I always go back to two guys who were rising seniors when Steve Logan became the head football coach at ECU in 1992. Ernie "Sac" Lewis and "J Dog" Dillon were defensive players. These guys were solid Division 1 players. They both had a physical presence and most significantly had a very strong sense of commitment to the tradition of the program. These guys had aspirations of getting a shot at their next level but were not in a league with Peppers. They were coming off a 11-1 season and were upset with the way the head coach left. They were determined to perpetuate the success of the program. These guys were vocal every day. We lost a lot of great players to graduation, but they continued to grind. Transition is always a challenge and we ended up 5-6 that year. Logan would eventually become the all-time winningest coach in the school's history, and I really believe these young men were a significant part of his future success because they salvaged the culture. The culture was grounded in a level of commitment that produced overachievement and a very high expectation of mental and physical toughness.

When I think back through thirty-plus years of football seasons, the same names always come to the forefront. It's hard to forget those individuals who gave everything they had to give and demanded the same from those around them. We can think about traits such as mental and physical toughness, trust, loyalty, coachability and commitment.

What we always find is that the individuals we classified as leaders inevitably possessed all of those qualities.

We always expect the quarterback of a football team to possess leadership qualities. That individual is expected to have a deep knowledge of the game, the ability to execute, toughness, and durability. Those who can successfully produce "big" plays under duress earn the respect of their teammates, and with that respect those teammates acquire they feel a willingness and a possible obligation to sell out at a higher level for the cause. They become even more dedicated to being fundamentally sound, because they believe that if they do their job, their leader will find a way to make it happen.

I've seen this happen with a number of individuals, like Jeff Blake, David Garrard and T.J. Yates, all of whom have had successful NFL careers. Marcus Crandall, Darian Durant and Shane Carden didn't make it to the NFL, but they played at the next level in Canada or arena leagues, and all of them have been significant leaders. All six of these men had a great sense of command, could take a hit, and were willing to run with the football when necessary. Garrard not only ran the ball but ran over defenders on frequent occasions. Carden had a similar type of savvy and toughness. The power of leadership at the quarterback position has been very well established throughout the history of football. It is certainly a good place to start when we consider the type of individuals we seek to recruit who will direct the future of the program for years. It is a natural position to serve as a cornerstone for peer leadership.

Defensively, for whatever reason, if someone is to emerge in a leadership role, it is usually a linebacker. Linebackers are seen as directors of the defense. They make the defensive calls and usually possess exceptional explosive qualities as well as size and strength. This position group would probably be the best choice to represent the team in a street fight, but defensive linemen, particularly defensive ends, have also become most impressive physically over the past decade.

This is where you typically look to find your "dogs" who can lead their peers with toughness and grit. Stature is going to be a factor, and the key is to find the personality and commitment to go with it. There is no playbook for developing peer leadership on defense. The offseason program will be a great indicator of who might rise up and assume that role. Coaches can quickly identify these individuals through their hard work ethic, competitive nature, personal intensity and desire to improve. I believe that it is crucial that you find these types of players, particularly considering the list of challenges we face today with teaching the value of the team over the individual.

Leadership Principles from the Marines

Several years ago, I began to bring Marines in to speak to our players about the fourteen leadership principles of the Marine Corps. I found that the in-season portion of the red-shirt developmental phase was a particularly good time to educate those individuals who had been assigned to the "developmental squad" — a mix of walk-ons, late bloomers and redshirted freshmen scholarship players. We train early on Friday mornings with these players, and the Marines were gracious enough to drive two hours to be there at 6 a.m. They would then "hang out" after speaking to the team and continue to talk to our players during the workout. Of course, the leadership principles of the Marines are very similar to the principles we relentlessly drill into our athletes. When they begin to understand the way that these principles apply to life and death situations, there is an impact. Real life stories of uncommon valor do make a difference.

Knowledge

The starting point is always the vital importance of "knowledge." Marines talk about the range of knowledge that you acquire, as well as the knowledge that is required before you can be referred to as professional. Football players who have average talent, but what you might consider professional knowledge, accomplish incredible levels of success. T.J. Yates was booed during football games, and even once at a basketball game he attended. He ran a 5.0 forty on a good day. He wasn't strong, but he was smart and he knew the offense inside out. He demonstrated the power of what was between his ears through his senior season and made it in the NFL for a number of years. You must learn to master your trade, whatever position you play. Sit down with your position coach. Stay in the film room. Study the opponents in your conference and what they do. Spend extra time on fundamentals. Master every situation in your mind.

Bearing

Another principle that I believe has important significance is bearing. This is an area that needs to be addressed more frequently and consistently enforced. The Marines list three areas of focus—carriage, appearance, and personal conduct. Basically, we are referring to representing your organization with class. Every member of the organization is representing that organization the same way and would be offended to see anyone representing it in a different manner. This expectation should be explained in great detail throughout the indoctrination process. The standard is a favorable impression at all times. One example would be the way the team travels. You can recognize a great deal about a football team by the way they travel and prepare for an away game. It should be viewed as a business trip. My father did not allow the team to speak on the way to an away game, and I did the same thing with my wrestling team. Of course, these were bus trips, and not overnight. If you lost, you also did not speak on the way home.

Collegiate trips are overnight and typically have a rigorous schedule of events, including meals and meetings. The majority of these trips are plane flights that include staff, players, cheerleaders, administrators, and boosters. There is a high level of opportunity to lose focus with so much going on. If you compromise the standard of the way your team travels, you will have players sleep in, show up for meetings late, become obsessed with their cell phones, and violate curfew. In my opinion, the standard that collegiate football teams maintain with regard to bearing leaves a lot to be desired. No, you don't have to travel in a suit and tie and pretend to be Wally Cleaver, but everyone needs to represent the program the same way. We used to prohibit facial hair and earrings on road trips, and that has been kicked to the curb for years. Young athletes want to find a way to express themselves as individuals. It might show up in the form of different socks or shirt or shoes. It might show up on the field, where you make a call and a player does his own thing.

I believe that this disease will progressively cause a team to deteriorate from the inside out. There is a reason that military organizations hold appearance and conduct at a premium. If there is a breakdown in those areas, the problem is going to grow like a wildfire and inevitably raise its ugly head on game day. Unfortunately, I have to say that many of the coaches I've been around just don't get it. They fail to see the value of conducting a daily battle toward enforcing those little things all the time, every time, with consequence. Sometimes I think I must be really old. I find support, however, in the fact that the Marine Corps is also really old, but they have not waivered on the vital importance of bearing from top to bottom. If it ever changes, we should fear the result. Narcissism can indeed be cancerous. Never forget it. Sometimes really old ideas are still really important and reflect the fabric of America.

Endurance

The next principle that always proves to be vital to collegiate football players is endurance. That word goes a long way and carries with it a multiple set of applications, both physical and mental. The perspective on being in great football shape is always interesting, and standards are forever changing. I believe you need to run the hell out of everyone all the time, and I will stand by that. You can engrave it on my gravestone.

The type of running you wish to incorporate into your program is always a conversation based on the experiences and background of the football staff. Football players are generally soft when it comes to standards of conditioning within the collegiate realm.

Military personnel, on the other hand, have traditionally run too much. In recent years, they have begun to do less longer aerobic running and more anaerobic interval type work and even some speed training. In boot camp, they are still going to run you into the next century, and I have often given that fact some serious consideration for freshmen. I think they need to run like hell just for the sake of finding their toughness threshold and consequently find the effort it takes to raise it. You can go down the street and find people in good enough shape to play football. Playing the game and dominating the game are two different mindsets. We use 20 x 110s as a test on reporting date. I have used a 4 x 300 yard shuttle with 25 yard increments and a one-minute rest. That was pretty tough. Of course, the times required are a very significant factor as well. The bottom line is that we do a ton of running leading up to reporting day and mix it up quite a bit to keep it fresh and keep people guessing.

Endurance training is also going to include the manner in which a player handles the competitive season. Football is a game of collision, and it is very true that athletes are bigger and faster. Big people traveling fast cause damage, sometimes to themselves. Injuries are sometimes inevitable, but also to a certain extent preventable, and the athlete must be resilient. Football is definitely a game in which almost everyone on the playing field is experiencing some level of pain in his body. Every time I woke up the day after playing a collegiate football game, I felt like I had been hit by a train. You had to start preparing your mind for the next game and bring your body along as quickly as possible. Twelve weeks of that is cumulative. The word endurance would include durability. That is a word I like to use when speaking to scouts: "This guy is durable."

Another way to view the concept of endurance is by considering the entire collegiate career. I've seen many different scenarios that include major surgery and extensive rehabilitative processes. Probably the most frequent incidence of injury that we see that requires a long, extensive rehabilitative process is the anterior cruciate tear. In my opinion, it is a two-year process to get back to total full speed capacity, but some might disagree. I've seen 85-90 percent after one year, but never 100 percent. It is a tough injury, and you have to get your mind right and pour yourself into rehabilitative mode with great tenacity. Larry Shannon was a receiver I coached who is probably the best example of an athlete that experienced this injury and was able to grind it out and ultimately spend some time in the NFL. Larry was one of those people who comes immediately to mind when you are thinking about former players with leadership qualities. Larry was a very hard worker and actually worked his way into a 44" vertical jump, which is a school record and an almost unbelievable feat after experiencing an ACL tear. Funny how people with leadership qualities do great things as individuals as well. That's the way it usually rolls in the world of collegiate athletics.

Integrity

A leadership principle that we can spend a lot of time talking about is integrity. Often the new rookies entering the program cannot provide you with a definition, which is unfortunate. They only know it has something to do with telling the truth. In defining integrity and the ways that it might apply to one's collegiate football career, it is important that an athlete understands that he must possess sound moral principles. I always like to explain to our athletes that they have a responsibility to themselves as elite athletes. The collegiate population sometimes practices very unhealthy habits, like lack of sleep, alcohol abuse and placing oneself in environments that can be troublesome. An athlete must have a moral compass that directs them in a manner that points north. Elite athletes have to make sacrifices to remain at the top of their game.

We are progressively learning more about the values of sleep, and we now know that alcohol certainly has no value in the life of a serious athlete, particularly if it becomes excessive. Making the right choices falls in the integrity category. The ability to be honest with yourself about the importance of sacrifice will no doubt contribute to the benefit of your career. The ability for you, as a young man, to tell yourself the truth about yourself can go a long way. You are aware of your weaknesses on and off the field and you strive with great effort to develop those weaknesses into strengths. You are also honest with those who are there to make you better and influence your life. You want to be worthy of their trust. Coaches need to convey to their position group that the athletes can come to him with anything that is truthful and that there will be a strategy to get it fixed.

Unselfishness

Obviously, with all that has been said referencing this generation, we certainly would include the principle of unselfishness in our toolbox of Marine Corps leadership principles. There are situations that arise every single day in the life of a collegiate athlete when they can decide to think about themselves. If you are not academically eligible and you are playing a significant amount of snaps, you have damaged the team. Depth is always an issue, and experience is another key consideration. If you are starting left tackle and you don't go to class, the consequences of your level of undisciplined behavior are going to affect everyone. There just aren't that many exceptional left tackles in the world. You will hold the team hostage to your ignorance. If you have several previous years under your belt as a starter, the damage is more severe.

When I look at the depth chart, I look at the top three individuals in every position. They are significant and must be similar in talent; otherwise, we have no depth and we are an injury away from failure in that position. Unselfishness sometimes includes the recognition of your own value to the team. You learn to play with pain and play through pain because of your commitment to your teammates. I have heard stories of Marines in gun battles who were wounded and would hide that fact because they didn't want to stop fighting and abandon their brothers in the corps. Playing with an ankle sprain or muscle strain is tough, but not that tough, my brother. It's worse to abandon your teammates in a crucial game.

Dependability

Dependability, without a doubt, is one of the most important principles for our players. This principle could be included under the heading of a few other principles. The Marine Corps keeps it separate, and it is not difficult to understand the reason. You can fall short, but if you are dependable you will always have the opportunity to rise up and succeed. My favorite player that I always mention, because he was such a great example of this, was Duane Ledford. Duane is currently the offensive line coach at North Carolina State University. Here was a young man who came into the program under 250 pounds, and no one could figure out what position he should play for several years. He started out as a defensive player—kind of like a "tweener" linebacker/defensive lineman. He didn't seem to be able to excel at any one position, but he had a relentless work ethic and played hard on every snap, every day. He trained like a monster and loved the weight room. He was dependable at the highest level 24/7. It was in his DNA. He could have become frustrated at some point and gone the other direction. Duane worked so hard that he gained 60 pounds and got faster.

Duane's senior season was one for the Guinness Book of World Overachievement, if such a book existed. He started at offensive line, and he excelled with the help of an excellent coach named Steve Shankweiler. He had such a great season that he would afford himself an opportunity to play in the NFL for several years. There is no doubt that his success as a collegiate coach falls in line with his level of dependability in going the extra mile as a coach every day as well.

After many decades of being around this game, I really believe that dependability frequently overrides talent. Talented athletes who make mental mistakes in crucial situations will give up big plays or prevent big plays from being executed, and as a result will quickly kill a football team's success on any given afternoon. I would take a player with exceptional dependability and less talent over the alternative every time. People commonly talk about how you should play the game for the guy on your right and guy on your left. That has everything to do with dependability, and thereby being mentally prepared. This is also another place where we re-emphasize the importance of knowledge. It is impossible to be dependable without knowledge.

Enthusiasm

There are many ways to define the trait of enthusiasm and the power within that word. I like to think about the individuals who I've coached over the years who possessed that trait, because they create positive energy in their mere presence. You need those people around, because you are always going to have challenging situations that threaten morale. Those individuals who remain vocally positive and display high energy in every circumstance are valuable assets to a team. During several years of successful seasons, we had two players who were perpetually energized and positive, whatever the situation. Their names were Jerome Barnwell and David Burnell. These two friends were very strong Christians and carried themselves as if they were seasoned veterans in overcoming the challenges of life. These guys were walk-ons who loved to work hard and had fire around them that burned consistently every day. They were uplifting to their teammates, whatever the situation, and always willing to pray for answers as well. David's nickname was "Flea." He was about 5-foot 3-inches tall.

After graduating, David joined the Marines, and is still enlisted as far as I know. Jerome became a fitness trainer. I'm sure these men are still enlightening everyone around them with their energy levels.

Although they did not get to play many snaps throughout their careers, they assumed an important role in helping the team overcome adversity. Everyone recognized their deep commitment to their faith and the impact that this dynamic duo had on our team.

There are many ways to express enthusiasm. Sometimes it can simply be expressed in the way you play the game, and I'm not referring to a celebratory end zone dance. We had a running back from Neptune, New Jersey named Scott Harley. Scott would not impress upon you that he was an enthusiastic person with excellent social skills. He was relatively quiet, and he would sometimes even get into fights with teammates. But Scott demonstrated a high level of enthusiasm by the way he played the game. Not only did he demonstrate it himself, but also motivated the entire home crowd in the stadium to get involved as well. Scott had a high level of natural lower body strength and a low center of gravity. This made it very difficult to get him on the ground. He would run with second, third and fourth effort and always run for more positive yards than expected. His effort was so recognized that the crowd would chant his name. Of all the players I coached, he is the only one for whom I ever witnessed a chant from the stands in unison. His enthusiasm was expressed from the inside out without uttering a word or performing a touchdown celebration dance. It was great to see.

I don't think anything good happens when there is negative energy. We almost always have a group to train at 6 a.m. each morning. People have just gotten out of bed, and it could be ugly if you don't get it going and have a fast start. Coaches need to be ready to set the climate with great energy. There will be plenty of individuals who will be happy to simply trudge through the workout at that hour. You must set the tempo and make sure they understand the expectations. When that drill sergeant begins a day with his trainees during boot camp, it is a lightning fast start. There are no questions about the expectations.

Initiative

Probably the final Marine Corps leadership principle that factors into peer leadership and must be included in our toolbox would be initiative. The specific methods of taking initiative as a player require creativity. I have seen meetings called by players that usually have a special purpose of "concern." Many times, it is a senior group taking the initiative to reinforce something that has been addressed by the coaching staff. It might be a power move by the seniors to express the expectation they have of the underclassmen that falls in line with tradition. There may be a feeling that current behavior is subpar to established standards. Players might also take the initiative to simply motivate themselves. We are always looking for them to try and address their weaknesses through extra work.

The second type of leadership to be considered is the coach-to-player relationship. In order to optimize the power of that relationship we must first have a tradition, an ethos and a mission. There is a quote that speaks to the ethos of the Marine Corp that was stated by T.R. Fehrenbach in *Leading Marines*: "Marine human material was not one whit better than that of the human society from which it came. But it had been hammered into form in a different forge, hardened with a different fire."

Building Traditions

Collegiate football programs have carried a special identity, and many institutions have certainly established traditions. You don't hear much about an ethos, but it strongly exists within a program that has had the same coach and a large degree of success over an extended period of time. We can think about people like Woody Hayes, Bobby Bowden, Steve Spurrier, Bo Schembechler and a number of others who would fall into this category of building collegiate football dynasties. These types of programs have progressively established strength in tradition and uniqueness, and they have accomplished the mission largely because of the personality and methods of their head coach. The institutional traditions built over time are also carried forth and blended into the athletic program and strengthened by every great athletics director and coach as well. There are strong parallels with these types of programs and military leadership foundations.

Unfortunately, in today's football society, coaches are not at one school for long unless they are consistently winning at a high level or resistant to being offered a fortune to go somewhere else. Coaches who remain in a program and a tradition over time have an opportunity to make the experience very special to the student-athlete, and hopefully that is where their interest is established first and foremost. I'm not sure of the number of athletes that would use the term "calling" for their choice of university, but the right coaches can certainly help create that type of commitment over time. The Marines refer to the emblem of the eagle, globe and anchor being "tattooed on the soul." They are very much invested in a "rite of passage" as the standard of being able to refer to themselves as a United States Marine. You must pay a price to become a member. When your football team develops a feeling even similar to that type of passionate commitment, you will win games. I've seen it firsthand.

When we refer to a rite of passage into a collegiate football program, the new player begins with reporting to summer camp and learning to adapt to the tempo and speed of practice and the game at another level. There is going to be an elevated expectation of gaining knowledge and adapting to a new level of mental and physical toughness. The freshman will experience competition with individuals who have greater talent along more size, speed and strength. The collisions will be more violent. It will be much more challenging to be as dominant as some have been at the high school level. Fortunately, in today's experience, you see very little activity that could be classified as "hazing" during that adjustment period for new players.

In my experience, I've seen collegiate athletes gain respect and acceptance by the way they play the game and the physicality they bring to the table. Programs that project distinguishing characteristics that categorize their athletes as "different" are somewhat rare, but they certainly do exist. I was recently watching the NCAA National Finals in wrestling. One of the Penn State wrestlers secured an incredible victory over an Ohio State opponent that ended up giving Penn State the national team title. When interviewed, the young man stated, "That's what we do at Penn State. We win national titles and we win national team titles." He is certainly correct. The program has racked up seven national titles in eight seasons. Winning establishes certain traditions. Whatever the players and coaches believe has contributed to consistently winning national football titles at Alabama is going to stick. Success builds tradition. An ethos begins and then continues to take shape. People discover what binds them together, and they begin to build an identity.

There is a story from July of 1950 when the 1st Provisional Marine Brigade was rushing to Korea to assist the Army in stemming the North Korean tide. In August, a British military observer desperately fighting in and around Miryang sent the following dispatch: "The situation is critical and Miryang may be lost. The enemy has driven a division sized salient across Naktong. More will cross the river tonight. If Miryang is lost..will we be faced with a withdrawal from Korea. I am heartened that the Marine brigade will move against Naktong Salient tomorrow. They are faced with impossible odds, and I have no valid reason to substantiate it, but I will have the feeling they will halt the enemy…these Marines have a swagger, confidence and hardness…upon this thin line of reasoning, I cling to the hope of victory."

The following morning, the Marines attacked under the close air support of Marine gull-air corsairs. Two of the lead battalions undermanned, "thin rifle companies pushed across the open rice fields," and "up the steep ridge. Three times the Marines reached the top; three times they "were thrown back. The fourth time, they stayed."

The Marines faced a night of repeated infiltrations and a series of hard attacks. As dawn approached, it became evident that the Marines were there to stay, and by daylight, the communist retreat became a rout. "When night descended again…the only North Korean left in the Naktong Bulge were dead ones amid the flotsam of a wrecked division. Thirty-four large caliber artillery pieces were taken by the brigade… enemy casualties exceeded 4000." The "thin line" carried the day, not because they had strength in numbers or fire power; they carried the day because they were Marines.

The stories of early triumphs and uncommon valor throughout the history of the Marines has progressively established a rock-solid tradition. Success always stems back to the courage and actions of individuals within the organization. The U.S. Marine is described as having experienced a "personal transformation" during the training process which provides a sense of "service, honor and discipline." They together develop a "sense of brotherhood, interdependence and determination to triumph." In athletics we sometimes talk about confidence being born through demonstrated ability. This is undoubtedly very true, but confidence must also be rooted in training and tradition, as it is in a military organization.

When you are a new coach around a program for only a brief period of time, it becomes very challenging to instill a tradition. It's hard to lead something you haven't ever really been part of. I remember experiencing a transition of a coaching staff, and it was interesting to me that the incoming staff was spending extra time learning historical facts and the words to the fight song in two weeks' time. Military organizations such as the USMC are sustained upon decades of tradition. Marines have the advantage of a lifetime career to develop leadership qualities. Leaders can be built over time, because a military career can be viewed as a process. Elements of the ethos are seen as intangibles, and leadership philosophy is viewed as tangible. The Marines list tangible elements as "core values, leadership traits and principles, the oath that all Marines take when assuming officer or enlisting and special trust and confidence." Leaders are going to have to understand how all of these elements fit together. The concepts behind them provide direction to the leadership.

Core Values as Building Blocks

When considering the structure that a coach aspires to build his team upon, these foundational tenets are vital. Imagine first building your team on the set of core values that your program views as the keystone. Marines talk about these core values as serving to "buttress the structure which Marine leaders draw upon." As a coach, you must consider the tradition of the program and the core values that you want to live by in building your "blocks in the arch, each depending on the other." Remember millennials traditionally have a major issue with deeper and more sustained thought.

Finding Our Leaders

If the world believes that leaders can be developed, we should characterize the types of individuals that we hope to target as potential leaders in our program. We should seek out individuals with great energy and dependability. We should ask ourselves if this individual understands the importance of being on time, and are we able to count on him in every situation? Will he take responsibility to learn the game of football at a very high level? Can he remain focused on a deeper task? We don't want a track record of absence and lateness, and high school coaches should be able to provide that information very accurately. These types of individuals reduce the impact of their trustworthiness by at least 25 percent in not being responsible. They set a bad example, and they can potentially be at the root of a disease. They are extremely difficult to change because they were late for kindergarten and kept showing up late every year after that.

They have a weak level of commitment, which is tied in closely with both dependability and responsibility. Spirit and dependability should be easily researched when interacting with high school coaches. It is always possible, however, that those coaches are not truthful.

To be a great model, the leader must also possess physical and mental toughness. You cannot be successful playing a game that involves frequent violent collisions without toughness. You don't want to recruit an athlete with talent who cannot play with pain and have a high level of durability. I always tell our football coaches that if they can sign people who have football skills and are willing to hit you in the mouth, I can make them better. Physicality is crucial. I believe that you can earn peer respect with your helmet and shoulder pads.

Dependability, energy and toughness are all included in my list of vital characteristics of our leaders. The last one I will mention is loyalty. Loyalty has been discussed in detail, however, there is a special type of loyalty that I feel must exist within the heart of the athlete. The athlete needs to be in touch with the tradition of the athletic program and also possess an appreciation for and dedication to the head football coach. There are always obstacles and issues to deal with in the daily occurrences within a collegiate football program. Sometimes there are mountains to climb, and when things become challenging, strength in loyalty is what is going to hold things together. When people start to blame each other and not take ownership of the issues, things start to unravel. When players bail on the head coach, things can get very ugly, particularly if they are credible. When a coach extends a young man a scholarship, that young man needs to have an allegiance to his coach. Not a whole lot more than that should need to be said.

There is another military trait that has very strong application to athletics and certainly worth talking about. It is referred to as adaptability. We previously discussed the concept of friction. The collegiate player is going to have to learn new systems and schemes.

He will lose and gain teammates. He may have a different position coach every year. He may have a new head coach. He must adapt to the speed of the game. Where performance training is concerned, he may have to adapt to something new every three weeks. Moving away from home and moving into a college dormitory is an enormous change in itself. We must help our athletes adapt to many situations so that they maintain a clear focus without distraction.

Transformational leadership is the most popular and most studied form of leadership. This form is utilized for transforming groups during times of change. It is also noted for inspiring high levels of performance. This is the type of leadership a head coach would be looking for as he takes over a program. The individual sets forth a compelling vision and an alignment of goals that connect with those who must follow. This is referred to as individualized consideration. The coach must have charismatic qualities that inspire and move people into action. This person is a role model who walks the talk. He will challenge the innovative nature of his staff. The Transformational Leadership Institute, founded by Orlando Reyes, offers a program designed to give head coaches a roadmap to success.

Attempting to motivate young athletes by providing them with a feeling of ownership might be a delicate process, but it still remains possible as long as the leader maintains the level of standards required to sustain a disciplined environment. The word that you see in this form of leadership is inspiration— to inspire others to accomplish specific process goals with energy and enthusiasm. Another term of primary importance is vision. I think that vision is a great concept as long as you understand that not everyone has 20/20 and some need glasses to see things perfectly. Whatever the vision, everyone understands the incredible amount of work in the process that it takes to get there.

Teaching Leadership By Modeling It

The personality characteristics of the leader are crucial to the effectiveness of the process that brings the group toward the vision. The coach invests a deeper level of thought to the words he speaks and how those words are perceived. He must be confident and speak with energy. His underlying objective is to transform the interests of each individual into the interests and identity of the team. This objective goes back to promoting a set of core values and character traits set forth as the foundation. I see this method being highly dependent upon the strength of character and charismatic qualities of the head coach. Many would hope that the millions of dollars now invested in that individual would certainly encompass the existence of just those qualities. At the time he is hired, that individual must represent and have a plan for the changes that must occur for a higher level of success. Transformational leadership is just what it says. Everyone from the top down, and through the organization, is buying into the mission and supporting each other with like-mindedness.

It is fairly evident that the leadership of a collegiate football team is trait-oriented. One man runs the show, and he is now earning millions of dollars because of the personal traits that he has exhibited and influenced others with throughout his career. It's all about his abilities, and he receives credit or criticism based upon his integrity, skills with people, and ability to motivate others to sell out for the cause. Wins or losses determine his destiny, no matter how great people might believe he is as a husband, father, Christian or philanthropist.

The third type of leadership relevant to the success of the total program is the leadership necessary to optimize the performance of the staff. I can attest to this first hand, since my own staff has continued to grow over the many years I've been a department supervisor. As a leader, this is where you start to become aware and in touch with the type of power and influence you have on the perspectives of the individuals who report to you. As a leader I have always preferred that those individuals view my influence within a certain light so that I might better serve them, and I have also wanted to project a high level of integrity toward the execution of our common objectives.

I have always believed that sharing information with others who are working with me or on my behalf is important to their success and our collective success. There is a continuous flow of new information circulating through our profession. It is important to continue to learn information if it will have an impact on the effectiveness of your staff, and therefore the program. Just like most professions, we have a certification process and then a process of continuing education units per year to maintain our certification. Some people view the whole process as a scheme for the national organization to boost its source of income; nevertheless, someone must be responsible for organizing and perpetuating the profession. A good leader needs to facilitate the continuing education process for his staff. Personally, I like to conduct my own clinics, whereby I have some control over the choice of topics that are relevant to the current needs or preferences of the staff. People cannot grow without information.

As an effective leader, you must have a high level of mastery within your field. It may be referred to as expertise. People are looking toward and expecting to learn from you. As a director of a department, I have never felt that I have enough expertise. I have always felt that I needed to attempt to gain as much information as humanly possible to stay ahead of the game. This level of mastery must not only be demonstrated through discussion; your staff or subordinates need to see the knowledge in action. They must be able to learn to coach by watching you coach.

2nd Platoon 1st Force Reconnaissance Company, USMC with General Mattis (now SecDef), Camp Rhino, Afghanistan December 2001.

"Mission first, Men always."
By John Dailey

The Marines place an incredible emphasis on leadership. From the first days in boot camp, long before I had anyone to lead, the importance of leadership was beat into my head (mostly figuratively, but sometimes literally.) Specifically, we were taught the following leadership traits, using the acronym JJ DID TIE BUCKLE:

Justice, Judgment, Dependability, Initiative, Decisiveness, Tact, Integrity, Enthusiasm, Bearing, Unselfishness, Courage, Knowledge, Loyalty, and Endurance.

These are the traits of a leader. We are charged not just with memorizing them, but understanding them, and living them. In the Marines leaders often ask for an opinion as to which of these traits is most important and which is least important. Maybe the best answer is that they are all equally important, but I have always felt and have always answered that tact is the least important. If I were a politician I would answer differently but, thank God, I'm not. It's not that I don't find tact important, just not as important as the others, and quite often we mistake the use of tact for just not saying things that need to be said. As far as the most important, for me, it will always be dependability. If you know you can count on me, not usually or sometimes, *but without fail,* than you will trust me as a leader. In fact, I think that many of the other traits listed are component traits of dependability. Leaders can't be dependable if they are not knowledgeable, loyal, just, and courageous. If I can't trust your judgment or integrity, I obviously can't depend on you.

The circular question we struggle with is which is more important; the mission or the men? Everything we do has to be in service of mission accomplishment. That's our job. But, if you don't take care of the men they won't be there to accomplish it. The truth is, in most cases, by working towards one of these, you take care of the other. Treat the men like men, give them room to grow and the education and training they need to be successful, look after them and look out for their welfare, and they won't let you down. In fact, in most cases, I think you'll find they exceed your expectations.

One of the tough things is that looking out for your men often means making them do things they don't want to do. Sometimes long hours are necessary. Pushing them outside their comfort zone is needed for them to grow. You have to give them room to run, but you must also hold them accountable for their actions and not be afraid to pull in the leash when they run too far or in the wrong direction.

CHAPTER SIX
ESPRIT DE CORPS

Esprit de Corps is defined as a group of individuals working together with energy, enthusiasm and a level of pride toward the good of the group. It is related to spirit. It is a disposition of the mind. It is about assertiveness. It is viewed as animating or life giving. Taken from the French, it literally means, "the spirit of the body."

One of the first times in my life that I experienced this on a personal level was when I was in grade school and went on a retreat that was related to the Christian walk. I was probably in fifth or sixth grade. There were a number of activities and a rigorous schedule that included meditation and prayer. In a moment, following a speech from one of the brothers in the monastery, I remember a feeling of joy and energy as I felt chills run through me. It was emotional. I wanted to raise my hand, or maybe jump up and yell out something. My young mind was overwhelmed with the belief that Christ was alive in me, and I remember that for several days I thought I was being called. I didn't quite answer, but I will not forget that experience.

If the Holy Spirit has an overwhelming effect, then I have to believe that on that day, I had an encounter with an empowering force that would cause me to maintain enthusiasm throughout my whole life, whatever the circumstances. It is not hard to get animated or feel a fire in your soul when you feel that God has a hand on you. The next day, as part of the itinerary, we played several baseball games and I remember they picked me as one of the All-Stars at the end of the day. I look back fifty years later and remember having a special feeling of confidence and peace. I believe

it was the power of the Holy Spirit, and it was one of the best days of my middle school life. You always perform better when you are relaxed and confident. I believe that I have carried that experience throughout my life. Becoming a man of the cloth would have probably saved me from a ton of issues, but God had a different plan for me. Regardless of my career path, the spirit never left me.

One of East Carolina's proudest moments. The 1992 Peach Bowl victory.

Around that same time, I started to accompany my dad to his summer high school football practices. As a head football coach, he stayed animated. This is where I started to learn the value of spirit and a positive attitude as applied to coaching. Any time my dad's players participated in drill work, there was constant chatter—almost like what you might hear at a baseball game as the pitcher gets ready to deliver a pitch. He always wanted to hear his players vocalize their enthusiasm so it could be recognized, along with their effort, through the drill work.

Another thing that was very apparent was the fact there was constant movement. Everyone ran from drill to drill and several individuals would try to be first in reaching the next destination. I don't think my dad ever paid much attention to talent and giftedness when he was in the initial stages of putting a team together. It was about finding tough, enthusiastic kids to come out and participate. The first thing they learned was spirit. He believed that there was tremendous power in the spirituality of an individual and even more incredible power within a group of individuals who collectively possessed this characteristic. Some folks believe that spirituality has to do with the power of the mind. That is exactly what my father was instilling in his teams, so that they might have the tools to overachieve. Then, with precision and passion, they were equipped to accomplish great things. People with spirit have an effect on others around them, and when the energy is greatly magnified a climate and a tradition begin to form.

A Spirit of Effort

When you talk about spirit as related to athletics, most people equate it to energy. Spirituality, however, has a number of deep implications that can strongly influence the individual. Spiritual people have a certain degree of mind control and self-confidence, because they are able to focus. A group of people with spirit can provide a sense of value and meaning to each other because of the excitement associated with their common goals and aspirations. That is why it is important for you as a coach to define the role that each individual has in contributing to the success of the group. My father made every one of his players feel important and take ownership in their role. It goes back to those two requirements common to someone who would contribute—hit and hustle. You could earn the right to be a member of the team with very little talent if you could do those two things. If you had great talent and couldn't do those two things, you probably had very little spirit about you, and your days were numbered. The individuals with low energy always take something very important away from the group.

Before I go on a different tangent about what I need to do to jerk a knot in the issues and deficiencies of the young people we deal with on a daily basis, I want to make reference to some of the things that I've had an opportunity to experience as a result of great efforts. I've been fortunate enough to be on the staff of sixteen bowl eligible teams. You don't get to a bowl without some great young men on your team. In my first year at East Carolina we defeated N.C. State in the Peach Bowl, and in my first year at UNC-Chapel Hill we defeated Auburn in the Peach Bowl. Strange coincidence, but great experiences. The players were incredible on both occasions. ECU ended up being ranked ninth in the country in 1991. That was special.

In my first year at UNC we played Florida State at home, and any time you got to look across the field at Bobby Bowden on the other sideline it makes you feel pretty good that you are simply there. I played college football at a smaller school in West Virginia, so I was very familiar with Coach Bowden. Everything came together for the Tar Heels that day. We won the game by a margin of 41-7. The players were incredible. I even got hit with a cooler of ice water, and that was very special as well. There was great spirit and celebration.

I have a lot of relatives who are full-blooded Irishmen and I grew up in a house with a full-blooded Irishman at the helm. I'm proud of my heritage and my family. When you grow up as an Irishman, you look at Notre Dame a little differently than any other program. It feels like a sacred place. When I was coaching at TMI Academy in Sweetwater, Tenn. we traveled there to play against their JV team back in the early 80's, and I went there to play the Irish again in South Bend when John Bunting was the head coach at UNC. After Butch Davis took the job, the Fighting Irish came to Chapel Hill and we delivered a victory to the Tar Heel faithful. That was a great day for me. It was another day when I had tremendous respect for the spirit and effort of our players.

The most significant sequence of events throughout my coaching career started when ECU started out of town toward Columbia, South Carolina to play Lou Holtz's Gamecocks and outrun a hurricane which was on its way to eastern North Carolina in August 1999. The Pirates came out of the game with a victory, but then learned that they would be stranded because of the flooding and devastation back home. We stayed in the hotel for the entire week and prepared to play a game against Butch Davis' Miami Hurricanes. Almost every starter on Davis' roster would be an NFL draftee of the future. It was going to be an enormous challenge, because Miami was also looking to vindicate a 31-6 loss that ECU had hung on them in Miami three years earlier.

Not only did we have to stay in a hotel for the week and train at a local Gold's Gym, we learned that we would have to play Miami in Raleigh at the N.C. State stadium. This would be another away game. The conditions in eastern North Carolina were disastrous. Many of the players had lost their apartments and all of their belongings in the flooding, so they had plenty to be concerned with beyond the football game. They also had a fan base that had been severely affected and needed something joyful to experience.

This game would be the most memorable day of my career. Our fans found a way to travel and packed the stadium. Our players fed off the emotion that began to generate long before kickoff. The Pirates fell behind early, but they roared back like a freight train in the fourth quarter. The result was a victory that was dedicated to the people who had suffered but, like the Pirates, would have the will to fight adversity and never know the meaning of quit. What the Pirates accomplished that night would go down in ECU history as an expression of what East Carolinians are all about. The players made it happen.

The Problem of Negative Spirit

The issue of subpar spirit is a glaring problem that debilitates a team and gets coaches fired on a frequent basis. In the last two decades I don't think I've been part of many teams without a person or persons with a negative spirit or what we might refer to as no spirit. It is certainly a huge distraction, and it impacts morale at a level that coaches sometimes fail to recognize. The spirit of your team is afflicted. No one sees this more clearly than the strength and conditioning coaches. You can beat your head against the wall trying to convince the head coach that he has a major problem, but you know you are already fighting the talent vs. compliance scenario. It is no mistake that the Marine Corps places so much value on esprit de corps as part of its culture. It is foundational to the pride and honor they share as being members of the organization.

I'm going to have to get up on my soapbox here and make a stand for coaches who have zero tolerance for narcissistic, selfish and non-compliant individuals who believe that they are above the standards and expectations placed on the team. Anyone involved in athletics can certainly recognize these types of individuals, and unfortunately, we probably see more of them associated with the game of football than other sports. We can all remember the kids in the neighborhood who could run and jump like a deer, look like they lifted weights but never picked up a barbell and had natural skills for most any athletic activity. Then, as they approached high school, they took a different road that led to a life of crime or drug abuse or depression. The rest of us would stand around scratching our heads, talking about the wasted talent and what we might have done with that talent if we could have been so lucky.

I think we also can remember coaches who have bent over backwards to try and save these types of individuals, particularly at the high school level while they might still be impressionable. I watched my dad do this for many years. He would recognize kids in physical education class who had talent and recruit them to play football. Some of the most talented kids had issues with their lives at home. It might have been anything from poverty to fatherlessness to abuse, or a combination of the above. I believe his level of success was probably higher than most in reaching some of these individuals. He provided transportation, daily counseling, financial support, personal use of his car, and anything else that might save a young man who was willing to practice hard and be accountable. That was the whole key. You had to maintain the standard set for the whole team.

He had a very special place in his heart for a young man who had it tough and still wanted to see the light. Just to know the young man would face problems every day when he went home from school was tragic, but he seemed to regard football practice as therapy, and he learned to take the coaching. The coaching was grueling, but his appreciation for what he was gaining was just as strong. There was no tolerance for anyone who wouldn't comply, because that was unfair to the team. The key was the coach's ability to educate kids with high talent and low accountability about the vital importance of an equal expectation from every member of the team. That's the only way you can have a group of individuals who can be referred to as a team. Otherwise, you are highly likely to fail.

If our responsibilities as coaches include the mission of changing lives and developing young people into better individuals with higher discipline, integrity and character, then what is the plan? Military organizations recognize that their plan impacts the fiber of America and the future and survival of our great nation. This is a high calling, and it is potentially a far cry from an attitude of, "Let's get enough talent to win enough games to get a better job and let the next regime deal with the issues we leave behind." I'm not advocating for anyone to take a job with that perspective, but I have witnessed it before. The financial landscape has drastically changed in collegiate football over the last decade. Successful head coaches are quickly becoming millionaires, and coordinators are not far behind. The level of financial appeal can be a game changer for the future of their entire family.

I don't think anyone doubts that the job is accompanied by incredible stress and high expectations, but the often-devastating effect on coaches' families can be overlooked. Coaches definitely earn their money. My point here is that coaches have a tremendous responsibility to their family as well as their career and can feel that they are in a double-bind situation. One thing that could help that situation is if they don't feel the need to micromanage their position group. When you look at the lists of student-athletes who have violated athletic department standards and consistently see the same names year after year, you realize that somebody needs to fish or cut bait. Sometimes I wonder why study hall still exists. For at least two decades, I have seen repeated lists of the same individuals within a program, who came late, left early, were distracted, on the internet or texting etc., etc. Study hall should be conducted within the football training facility with someone present who can administer punitive consequences for all of these offenders. I'm sorry, but I just don't get it. They need to give the study hall monitors a raise, or maybe just a daily bottle of scotch. They evidently are very tolerant, or perhaps very intimidated, individuals.

The Battle Between Spirit and Flesh

It only seems reasonable, when we are referring to spirit, to further study the implications of spirituality. I've heard many pastors and students of Christianity refer to a struggle between the flesh and the spirit. The flesh represents the submission to the temptation of worldly satisfactions. These temptations are easily identified and widely inclusive. The laws that we adhere to in the United States of America have been influenced by Christian principles, and we know that the founders of the constitution were likewise influenced. Fortunately, our currency still reads "In God We Trust," which is enough to stir my spirit because I believe in the power of God and the Holy Spirit.

The collegiate experience is one of incredible temptation. Athletes are highly visible individuals, and collegiate football players have competitive egos and a very strong desire to be recognized. The lifestyle is rampant toward sex, "the club", smoking weed, and any other fleshly endeavor that might propel them to the forefront of peer popularity. It really wasn't that much different forty years ago. You wanted the most recognition, the best-looking girlfriend, and a wild nightlife with your teammates in the most popular night club. Let's be honest, that's what most collegiate players do.

I will go to my grave with the belief that we practiced a lot harder than we partied back then, and I still maintain that the difference between then and now can be linked to that very fact. Losing a game hurt. It hurt bad. Nobody wanted to celebrate a loss. That was the only time you might not recognize a great spirit among us. I can say that we were all in it to win it. When we won, we celebrated hard, and when Sunday came, it was straight to business. We practiced and lifted hard all the time. If we would have sensed a weakness in the team commitment, it would have been addressed.

The reason I say "would have" is because I can't remember one. That's a fact. I remember losing people who didn't have talent or possibly had an issue; but I don't remember anyone who wasn't one hundred percent committed to the discipline, the work or the required accountability. You might say that at least a few players must have been using drugs. Maybe, but if true, they also had to be busting their ass while high on drugs. You might say that someone must have had an alcohol problem. Maybe, but not for that two hours a day when we practiced or trained. If it was game day, then they must have played without the negative effect of those addictions.

I hate to say that I believe today's collegiate football player shows a deficiency of spirit, but I've seen it too many times. The most common form is what we have previously identified as the "front runner"—the individual who does really well with winning and success, but struggles greatly when they are hit right in the mouth. If you have a number of those Individuals, you might be in real trouble, and it might be time to pass out resumes. Those front runners will have a strong sense of spirit, but only as long as they are winning and the process of winning doesn't become too mentally and physically challenging. These types if individuals can also become very creative with pain and discomfort.

They are subject to sustaining a hamstring pull, a severe headache or lower back pain that is difficult to diagnose.

The Bible speaks about losing the old man and putting on the new man. So, what is being referred to is making a choice to put aside all desire of the flesh. In other words, that old man becomes dead. The reason we put the old man aside is to optimize the power of the Holy Spirit within us. As long as we are making choices that are sinful and self-destructive, we are denying the spirit. We should not go through our lives allowing that old man to re-enter our decisions and inevitably hamper the calling and reward that God has prepared for us. This is a lot easier said than done for any human being on this earth, mostly because as humans we seek pleasure and we are easily influenced. As a collegiate athlete, worldly pleasures are abundant.

I truly believe that there is a connection between the power of the Holy Spirit and the perspective you have toward life every minute of the day. If you are living right, you are much more likely to feel spirited. You will be someone who demonstrates energy, enthusiasm and positive behavior. Keeping your spiritual life in order is going to provide you with a great opportunity to not only achieve, but to overachieve. You will also be more characteristically suited to lead others because leadership principles have biblical origin.

Many athletes within the ages of 18 and 22 are not ready to respond to biblical principles shoved down their throats because it never feels good to be convicted. Some young folks rationalize by adopting a perspective of saving themselves for change as soon as it becomes convenient. It is best to feed them a little at a time. The key is in the presentation.

Inspiring Spirit Through Effort

Organized football activities are designed to generate spirit through tempo. This is similar to military protocol in that folks are organized down to the minute and move rapidly. Any player who does not demonstrate spirit through effort is confronted. The drill must be repeated until the coaches are satisfied. As a strength coach, I always enjoy the tempo of practice, because people must fly around. This is the result of the recent revolution of the high tempo offense and the preparation to execute the high tempo offense on game day. I like anything that promotes a sustained elevated heart rate, with coaches demanding energy and execution at a very high level of expectation. Things have drastically changed over the years regarding the rigorous schedule and the demand associated with summer camp. You only have a certain number of practices available before you get into your first game week, and when I played in college we had three practices on most camp days. Those days are over.

Steve Logan hired Larry Coyer as our Defensive Coordinator in the early 1990s, and he brought in a camp schedule that they had been using at Ohio State. I thought that it was the best thing I'd seen since sliced bread, and it was great for generating team spirit. I think that there should be a mandate toward requiring that same schedule for every collegiate team, and it should go into effect immediately. This would solve all the current issues regarding safety and at the same time prepare the athlete to play football at the highest level possible.

This system is actually a three-practice-a-day schedule, so I know the first response is going to be knee jerk. But wait a minute. The first practice is actually forty minutes in duration. It is extremely high tempo, and it consists of the things you normally do at the beginning of practice with a shorter duration. The players know that this is practice is tough and demanding, but it ends quickly—with a long rest before the second practice. This first practice made the strength staff very happy, because it was very challenging from a conditioning standpoint. This is truly a time when you could say that the tempo of practice was actually contributing to the team's level of conditioning, because everyone's tongue was dragging on the ground.

Coyer's camp schedule provided a whole new perspective, because it wasn't your typical scenario of conditioning where, after everything else was completed, athletes start holding their backs or limping around to escape the discomfort. When the practice ended, the players went to the locker room, where food was available, and they could hydrate. They had time to ice or get treatment, but they would stay on site. There was also some meeting time as well.

The second practice would begin around mid-morning and would include what you would typically do in a regular period and team period. We went straight to pass skeleton, inside run drill, and other various situations where the team was divided up into certain sub-groups that would compete against each other in certain scenarios. The practice lasted slightly more than an hour, and the players stayed focus on the teaching. They knew that they would be off the field again in a short period of time and the teaching, the tempo, and the effort was excellent. It was the type of practice that would be greatly suited for the athlete of today. They could quickly get back to their cell phones and would not be forced into longer and deeper thought and concentration.

The players would then have an extended period to do nothing but rest. They were encouraged to go back to their rooms and sleep, and they seemed more than happy to follow those instructions. I think it brought joy to both players and coaches to know that when they stepped onto the field in a few hours for that final practice, they would be in a team situation for the entire duration. Team situations are more like the game itself and are competitive and fun, particularly if you love football. Your players enter the gate to the field already knowing that they are going to flex and go straight to team period, which promotes a great attitude from the jump. They also know that conditioning was taken care of during that first practice and unless they screw it up with mental mistakes and loafs, they will be finished as soon as team period is over. This third practice was about ninety minutes in duration. That camp was a happy and healthy camp. The players had time to recover and took the coaching. Spirit and morale stayed very high. This is just a perfect example of how you can maintain a very high spirit through innovative scheduling You are taking a number of psychological factors in mind and selling recovery. Your team knows that if they stay focused and go extremely hard that they will be provided time for recovery and an opportunity to re-energize.

That schedule was designed to provide the athletes with the best opportunity to recover, which meant that they would be more enthusiastic. In my opinion it worked beautifully toward that objective, but it was extremely productive as well. We need to know what we might take from this to make it more stimulating for the individuals who we coach on a daily basis . We also need to determine what type of environment do we need to -facilitate high energy.

Spirit Through Competition

One of the most powerful tools you have as a coach to generate energy is competition. There are many ways to set up competitive scenarios, and it can be a daily occurrence. I like to have a competitive finisher at the end of a workout. One example would be to have an offensive and defensive lineman execute a double kettlebell rack squat for one minute, touching their hips to a medicine ball at the bottom of the movement. If the defensive player loses, every defensive player in the group has to perform twenty up-downs. It always pays to be a winner, and there is always a consequence. There are of a ton of things you can do to end a workout competitively.

Another thing that I've done for many years is to draft testing teams. About a week before testing, we ask seniors to draft testing teams from the total roster. They pull a number out of a hat to dictate the order, and they are on a thirty-second clock for the next choice when their number is called. They might end up with nine people on their team, but we only take the top six scores for each test. Points are determined from the ten-point system we have established that is standardized to each position group and specific to each test. As we conduct the testing, we post a daily summary of the teams' scores.

This has been very good to us over the years in promoting team spirit. The team captains are motivated to make their team members accountable and also push their team to put forth one hundred percent effort, which is crucial to the validity of the testing. Because we are only taking the first six scores into account for each team, everyone from that team is able to contribute. For example, if we have someone who cannot perform a back squat, his score will be dropped, but he might still possibly contribute to the team score with other tests he is able to execute. We usually had as many as twelve teams and provided trophies for the first four.

Another way that you can promote peer accountability is to monitor class attendance and academic performance and incorporate those things into the scoring. The team might also be penalized when individuals are not doing things correctly. Any time we can somehow convince an athlete to confront his peers, we are promoting leadership. I believe that there is a movement within collegiate football to make things more "fun." I'm in agreement with workouts being more spirited, but I believe that military organizations established esprit de corps as a lasting foundational component—not something they have to strategize to recapture.

I see more strength and conditioning coaches try to identify with their athletes—what we might refer to as cheering more than coaching. It is not my style to dance up and down the sideline waving a towel as our team lines up for a kickoff, but I see such behavior becoming more popular among some teams that are currently successful. Sometimes things change. Sideline demeanor seems to be one of those things. I think enthusiasm is an effective driving force in most situations, so I've come to accept the behavior. Sometimes it is hard to accept actions that look more like fun over a demeanor that appears to be deadly serious. Approaches that produce winning sometimes change with time, but the key is the production of success. Every coach is different, and methods of motivating millennials and the individuals who fall into the Z generation are becoming more innovative and nonconventional.

Spirit Through Empowerment

The thing that we have to continue to remember in our mission to generate spirit is empowerment. We are attempting to strengthen and interject life into the individuals we influence every day. We must aim to be progressively unified as we continue to share the same passion for our common goals. Unity of spirit is the fuel that feeds high levels of collective performance. Understanding the full power of what potentially resides within us as individuals is a very deep topic. If we hope to tap into the full power of who we might become, it is my personal belief that we must adopt a biblical perspective.

When we examine scripture that speaks to the power within us as human beings, we should be encouraged about the incredible things that we might accomplish as believers. It almost seems to be ridiculously simple to access. All we need to do is recognize and accept the fact that we have a blessing available to us that provides us with the designed purpose of empowerment. We are empowered through the way we live and the way we interact with and serve our fellow man. When we realize that we have access to this awesome strength, we become highly energized and edified as we experience the gifts that become evident within us. We learn in Ephesians that we are able to fulfill through the spirit something exceedingly and abundantly above what we would ask or think.

I look at the young athletes that I interact with every day, and I see a variety of personalities and attitudes. I believe that their attitudes are impacted by the way they live and the influences that they experience. I always go back and think about the young men who earned Division I scholarships, but somewhere along the journey their choices and way of life turned them in a different direction. This is the reason that we need great people in the coaching profession. The spirit that exists within collegiate athletes can be extraordinary, if somehow it can be nurtured and unearthed. I am not advocating that we should become preachers of the gospel, but I am advocating for our responsibility to educate young men toward a way of life that gives them a chance to survive destructive influences. I have known many young individuals who I would describe as displaying a destructive spirit. I am going to continue to wear this out over and over again in every chapter of this book, because we have been losing people and it still continues.

Watching people underachieve and lose their future is as discouraging as it is encouraging to see someone with average talent make it to the NFL. It is discouraging, because you feel that they may never have an opportunity to do something great or learn the power that's available to them if they simply can make the right choices. In reality, disobedience has no excuses. There is always clarity and constant review of team rules and expectations. Disobedience in life causes you to be dead in the spirit. As an athlete, we as coaches recognize a certain darkness about athletes who underachieve. They don't listen when people talk to them. They seem to be distracted. Their effort is poor. They are not on board. The strength and conditioning staff is always keenly aware of these individuals, because like a drill sergeant we witness their every move, every single day.

Esprit de corps is not something that anyone within an organization can compromise. It only takes one person to begin to influence an organization in a direction of failure. These individuals must renew their mind to continue to be part of the organization, or they must be eliminated. We know that in this world as human beings, we battle a negative spirit. If you don't believe that your collegiate athletes battle this spirit, you will lose the battle for your job. You must stay on top of this battle at all times. We can talk about the salvation of men and the salvation of your program through the salvation of men. Becoming unified in the mission has a saving quality. You learn the value of spirit.

The Spirit of the Marines

I love the fact that Marines must do everything together and they know how to take care of each other. I wish we could go back to having a players' dormitory and dining hall and that it would be mandatory through their entire collegiate experience. We would know where to find them. We would know about their eating habits. We could quickly organize activities in a central location. They would have to learn to like each other and become a brotherhood. I believe that Ephesians 4:3 applies to everything we might do in this life. It states, "Make every effort to be united in spirit, binding yourselves together in peace. For there is one body, one spirit, just as you have been called to one glorious hope for the future."

You can argue that we are talking about two different types of spirit in this conversation, but I would beg to differ. Our intentions and hopes are directed toward the ultimate success for every young man in our program. We want them to live in the light. A quote from Thomas Ricks in his book *Making the Corps* really sums up the mission of those of us who deal with molding the future of young Americans. "I wanted to see how an organization could take fifty or so American kids—a group steeped in a culture of individualism, many of them users of recreational drugs, few of them with much education or hope of prospering in the American economy—and turn them into Marines who saw themselves as a band of brothers, overcoming deep differences of race and class. I wanted to see who would "make" it to the Corp, who wouldn't, and why. I also wanted to see how drill instructors would make them into Marines." He talks about the billboard sign that reads "Parris Island: Where the Difference Begins." Evidently a transformation is about to take place, and that transformation is going to include an education toward the value of a common spirit.

Some of the quotes that I've read from *Marine Corps Leadership* regarding recruits are amazingly similar to the thoughts I've had toward many young athletes. One of my favorites came from a staff sergeant named Rowland in his introductory directives. He stated, "Before we leave my island, we will be thinking and breathing exactly alike." This is one of the best statements I've ever heard regarding a zero tolerance for individualism. It is also reflective of the vital importance of unity of spirit. Elsewhere in *Marine Corps Leadership*, an officer named Sergeant Balenda states, "It's today's generation. They are raised by babysitters. There's a lot of broken families and they are doing their own thing on their own. My last platoon as a senior drill instructor, half the recruits came from broken families." Sergeant Carey says, "A lot of them have never been held accountable for anything in their lives. Here they begin to understand, and begin to rely on each other, which is what the Marine Corps is all about. That's the heart and soul of the corps."

This kind of assessment is very familiar. These are replicated thoughts in the world we live in with collegiate athletes. They have been coached and they have been exposed to individuals who have attempted to teach them values. If we consider the roughly 14 percent of recruits that washed out of Parris Island, we can compare that statistic somewhat accurately, with the individuals within a collegiate football program that requires us to work overtime to keep them in the boat.

When we talk about spirituality creating a "new man" or about making a decision to renew your mind, the objective is very similar to what military organizations endeavor to do in their approach. We want to clear individuals' minds of all the garbage and temptation toward self-destructive behavior—behavior that results in depression, darkness of spirit and failure. I don't think you can contemplate a strategy to build spirit within an individual or group of individuals without considering the power of the Holy Spirit. In military organizations, the indoctrination of values is a process of drilling and repetition. These values just happen to have their origin in biblical principles. If you want to be empowered at the very highest level of human existence and enlighten other individuals to follow in receiving this incredible gift, you will need to renew your mind. I'm referring primarily to coaches here, because the onslaught of influences that the collegiate athlete is clouded with is immense. You are going to have to renew your own mind and serve as a model to them. You will need a toolbox of methods that isn't always straightforward. As a coach, you don't have the luxury of conducting a boot camp while also brainwashing the trash out of the recruit.

Through your diligence and through your persistence with a plan, you can impact young lives beyond what you might even imagine. They will go beyond developing the "spirit" or "esprit de corps" that we refer to as necessary to the success of organizations and mandatory to winning football games. It may seem to be a Utopian objective, but it's worth every ounce of your effort to convince your team not to neglect their spiritual lives.

The process looks like this:

Ephesians 4:22-24

"Throw off your old sinful nature and your former way of life which is corrupted by lust and deception. Instead, let the spirit renew your thoughts and attitudes. Put on your new nature, created to be like God—truly righteous and holy."

Ephesians 5:8-9

"For once you were full of darkness, but now you have light from the Lord, so live as people of light" For this light within you produces only what is good and right and true."

Winning is an attitude! Put on the sword of the spirit!

Marine Corps Special Operations Command Detachment -1, providing security detail for Iraqi Interim government, 2004.

"The strength of the pack is the wolf and the strength of the wolf is the pack."

By John Dailey

The quote above is one of my favorites. It is from Rudyard Kipling's "The Jungle Book." I have always felt that it captures the essence of esprit de corps perfectly. I have got to be smart, strong, fit, and tough, because my teammates are counting on me to be. If you have a team where every member thinks this way, where everyone takes it upon themselves to ensure they are trained, equipped, and prepared for anything, then the team will be unstoppable.

The Marine Corps defines esprit de corps as the intangible spirit that lifts men above themselves for the good of the group. It also recognizes that no matter how well I prepare, there are going to be times that I will need support from my teammates. I need to know I can look to them for help without shame, because on another day someone else is going to need a hand and they know I'll be there to give it.

Developing esprit de corps requires a common goal, a shared vision, a culture within the team or organization that every member understands and can aspire to. In the Marines, esprit de corps is developed through shared hardship. In special operations units it begins with selection. My first experience with this was the Force Reconnaissance Indoctrination (known as Indoc). It was mostly physical: running, a lot of swimming, obstacle courses, then hours of running through the hills of coastal California, then down to the soft sand, carrying a fifty-pound ruck before they tell you to stop. After that it was a run into the ocean, choking down salt water and doing exercises in the surf zone. That's when people start to quit. Once one quits, it becomes contagious.

Finally, soaked and with sand in all of the places you don't want sand, you ruck back up and head back into the hills. By now there are only a few still going, with a truck following along behind. No one will try to stop you if you just get into the truck. My Indoc started with twenty-some soldiers, and only five of us finished the physical part. Then the testing starts, psychological, intelligence, and temperament. Finally the interview: "Why do you want to do this?" "What are some of your favorite books?" "What's your opinion on the political situation in the Philippines?" Then they give you the scenario, "You are leading a team conducting a desert observation post overlooking a village and a shepherd discovers your location. You can let him go and abort the mission, or kill him. What do you do?" In the end, only two of us were selected.

As much as the Indoc tested us, it also let us know what the culture of the unit was, what the men there believed in and placed value in, and what (if we wanted to join them) we needed to put value in. For the teams we ultimately were assigned to, it let them know that we understood these things, that we had paid the price of admission and earned the right to prove ourselves. In Marine Corps Special Operations we have a saying credited to SSgt Christopher Antonik, who was killed in action on July 11, 2010 in the Helmand Province of Afghanistan: "All it takes is all you got."

CHAPTER SEVEN
THE PLAN

The plan for success regarding collegiate football must, of course, begin with recruiting athletes. Unlike the military recruit, this experience for the athlete is going to be somewhat short-lived. Most individuals who choose to join a military organization are looking for a career. Similarly, every collegiate football player aspires to play professional football, but unfortunately that the opportunity is extremely slim. Where training and development are concerned, the athlete has a very short time to optimize his potential. Training is becoming more limited as programs continue to get hit with additional NCAA guidelines. Mandatory "off-season" periods are limited to approximately two seven-to-nine-week sessions a year. Any other training time that would be categorized as mandatory is actually "in-season," and not developmental. During mandatory, off-season periods the training is limited to eight hours a week, and other times during the year, the athlete can never spend more than twenty hours a week directed toward the total time committed to the football program.

Any strength and conditioning coach who has successfully survived this business for an extended period of time has likely instituted a sound training program that is going to achieve results. I have seen hundreds of young men improve their stature and physical performance just by merely showing up and working hard consistently over extended periods

of time. These results didn't come because I have been a magical strength and conditioning coach, but because we were able to ensure that the process was cumulative. We were afforded enough mandatory training time, along with the opportunity to educate the athlete toward the understanding of the importance of making every day count. They sprinted, jumped,

Praying that after 31 years, there is wisdom to accompany the white hair.

lifted and conditioned for consistent periods of time, and many of them loved to train because they wanted to be good.

As a head football coach, you must have the insight to understand that we do not have the same developmental situation that we had fifteen or twenty years ago. We have great resources and knowledge toward a sound nutritional program. We have incredible facilities and the technology to track our athletes' level of effort, workload and sleep. Unfortunately, what we have lost is mandatory, developmental training time, which is counterproductive. It is a fact, and because it is a fact, football coaches need to find athletes with a developmental background. They also need to find individuals who are closer to what they want them to look like when it's time for them to take the field on game day. It is increasingly difficult for us to put fifty pounds on someone with two seven-week mandatory developmental training phases in our arsenal each year. It can be possible, and I've seen it happen, but my point is that the changes have made it less probable.

Bringing in the Right People

I'm not sure how many people are going to take a strength and conditioning coach's perspective on recruiting to heart, but I'm going to throw it out there anyway. Collegiate football has evolved into a high-tempo, high-efficiency machine on offense. The tempo and physicality of the game have become weapons of choice. I see offensive schemes week in and week out that intend to confuse you, wear you down and prevent you from having enough time to adjust between snaps. Because of the effort required by defensive linemen to take on double teams, rush the passer and pursue the ball, a team needs to have three sets of individuals with similar talent to rotate into the game. I see this as a huge priority for the defense where recruiting is concerned. Defensive fronts can get shredded late in the game if the talent level or depth is suspect. Everything starts up front, so a team needs to prioritize a solid three-deep defensive line.

Defensively, it is also very evident that cover corners can make you a much more effective unit. If you have defensive backs who can "man" cover, you can bring more pressure. Being able to play more defensive players in the "box" provides you with a significant advantage in stopping the run and also puts more pressure on the quarterback.

Looking at the length of the yearly schedule and the statistical probability of injury, it becomes crucial to be "sixty-six strong". The twenty-two positions that make up the offense and defense must be three deep. Outside of those sixty-six slots, you have another nineteen scholarships to equal your eighty-five. That should take care of your specialists and provide you with an opportunity to super stack the crucial positions on both sides of the ball. I've never seen a recruiting class yet that was perfect. Sometimes coaches are going to miss. They may have been misinformed or possibly struck out on predicting the way that an athlete might develop.

Coaches can inherit programs that are severely lopsided and deficient in specific areas, necessitating an immediate and deliberate plan to correct these issues. The durability of a football team is a vital element of the success of any program, and as the physicality of the game intensifies, that element becomes an even greater challenge. Before we can consider the deeper requirements of a successful organization that involve the human dimension, we need a recruiting board with talented individuals stacked three deep in every position. We can then assess the strength of everyone's character. The primary theme of this book is to address the issues that don't show up on paper. We are attempting to further understand the strategies that we might employ to optimize the production of a collegiate football team. The objective is to bring everyone under a common set of values that define and fit the identity of the program.

One of the most glaring challenges of a new coach who takes over the reins of a program is the current roster. If there were discipline issues, they are still there. If there were talent issues, they are still there. Before you can begin to educate your own recruits, the previous roster must be re-educated. This can be a painless process or a very long, grinding experience. I've seen players recognize the need for change and view transition as an occurrence that will provide them with an opportunity for a more rewarding personal experience. On the other hand, if a team has been loyal to a coach who recruited them and nurtured them through their career, there will be challenges for the new regime. If the regime change was controversial and the coach who was on his way out had established some degree of success, there will be some significant hurdles to overcome. Sometimes the players are ready for a change and other times they remain committed to the previous cause.

It is interesting to me that administrative individuals often neglect the opinions of team members when considering change. If a coach is fired before the voice of the team is considered, the result can be a long and painful transitional process. The new regime will inherit a ton of issues that might have been avoided had there been some awareness toward the climate of the team. There's a long list of reasons behind the decision made by an athletic director to fire a coach, including the financial implications of a struggling program. It just seems reasonable to me to survey the leadership of the individuals who are required to go to battle on behalf of the program, rather than only consider the opinions of those individuals with super status but perhaps very limited insight.

Whatever the case, when we consider the human element of an organization, the mindset of the players factors into the equation. There must be a strategy to establish a new mindset or reshape the current climate. We need to remember that it is the human mind that facilitates quality of performance. Individuals outside the program may never recognize the empowering impact of a team thinking the same way about who they are and what they need to be successful.

Personal Factors Can Affect Performance

As a coach develops a roster of players, someone on the staff must do extensive homework on the family background of each individual. The number one factor that must be identified is the presence or absence of a male role model. Pastor T.D. Jakes expressed his feelings about the death of his father in a heart-wrenching memory that reflects the impact it had on his life.

"At sixteen years of age, I heard the slow creaking of pulleys that eased my father's cold body into the red Mississippi clay, and I learned that dead men can't talk and can't listen. I stood there with a thousand unresolved issues in my heart. Burning tears streamed down my face as I wept for my father. I wept for the questions I could not ask him. I wept for the grandchildren he would never see. I wept for the twinkle I would never see in his aged eyes. I wept for my mother who never married

155

again. I spite of his flaws, I wept for his attempt to provide, to love and protect us and for his tragedies. But most of all I wept for myself. Dad was gone like a gust of wind. He slipped through my fingers like sand. I clenched hard, but when I opened my hand, it was empty. He had slipped through the cracks and I wondered how he would leave without saying goodbye. Most of all I felt the pain of my father's absence as I performed on the football fields of life. I made touchdown after touchdown. I have heard the roaring of great crowds, but there was one face missing from the stands. I longed to hear one special voice above the roar of the crowd … but he was missing in action."

Pastor Jakes lost a father that he had known, and the deep expression of pain is clearly tragic. Many of the athletes that we coach within the realm of collegiate football either have not known their fathers or possibly chose not to know them. Personally, I don't think that their pain is much different than what has been expressed by Pastor Jakes, even though their fathers may be somewhere still alive. As long as we are going to keep talking about the power of the human element, we are going to have to devise a strategy to address this dilemma, targeting it with an extensive program of education, counseling, and mentoring.

The beauty of military organizations is that they have a method of erasing complicating factors by purging weaknesses, excuses and negative ways of thinking through intensive repetition and a focus on team versus self. They have well established processes for developing a brotherhood. I always tell our athletes that a brotherhood is different than a family. Sometimes families don't get along, and they don't have a sense of loyalty. A brotherhood is different. The members of a brotherhood must depend upon each other, and they learn to unselfishly give of themselves for the benefit of the group. When you look at the pictures of the groups of men in this book, you can almost feel the bond that they have among them. Obviously, they have been trained to commit to the ultimate sacrifice for one another. They are ready to sacrifice the entire life they have ahead of them for the cause. They are willing to train themselves hard and undergo incredibly high levels of stress to remain prepared.

The sacrifices and expectations for collegiate football players are much different than those for members of military organizations, but the value of an effective state of mind is very similar to both. That state of mind—a high level of physical, emotional, and spiritual health--is imperative if we are to expect the highest level of functioning when engaging in competition or combat.

Fatherlessness, drug and alcohol abuse, poverty and a lack of self-esteem are some of the factors that can seriously impact an athlete's domain of wellness. When I begin to interact with an athlete and observe his behavior and responses to specific situations. I am evaluating his "wellness." I am trying to determine if the individual is happy and enthusiastic. Does he demonstrate total wellbeing? This is one of the reasons we are now placing tremendous emphasis on nutrition and sleep. If you are not eating and sleeping properly, you are not well. You must be well to train and practice productively. You must recover. If you are not recovered, you will not be happy. Collegiate programs have now taken a word from military organizations called "readiness." Physical readiness is crucial to the development of the team. Athletes must be ready to work hard, and there can be no weak links in the chain. They cannot indulge themselves in the behaviors of some other students who might not be athletes. They must see themselves as different. Not better, just different.

Having a strong spirit is an integral part of one's total health. It is important to overcoming hardships and multiple forms of discouragement. Esprit de corps refers to the powerful spirit of the group, but is also important to consider the individual's personal level of spirituality as a coping mechanism. One of the frequent occurrences in athletics is injury. The need for shoulder or knee surgery arises frequently, and the injury itself can attack a player's spirit. The rehabilitation process requires a certain degree of courage and self-belief.

Measuring Wellness

I believe that the "wellness domain" within a football team is reliant upon and built upon social relationships. I think that there are many types of intertwined dynamics here. The way that an individual views his self-value or self-worth is going to have a heavy influence on his daily behavior. If his teammates have taken him in and have created a sense of fellowship and recognition, his life is going to be more enjoyable as an athlete. Many times, a football team will have small groups of individuals who hang out and go out together. One hundred people are going to have different interests. Some would rather live with one other teammate as opposed to a small group of teammates. Some will venture off into fraternity life. ECU had an informal football fraternity known as Foot Phi Ball. I liked that concept, because everyone knew they were part of the brotherhood just by becoming a team member.

Social media now serves as a barometer for self-image. I'm not sure how effective that is for an individual's sense of social health, but nevertheless it provides daily feedback. Young people take it seriously. A football staff should be skilled in making everyone feel a sense of belonging. Position coaches usually have their groups as guests for meals at their homes and do creative things to make them feel appreciated. Freshmen are adapting to being away from home and immediately get hit with a bundle of responsibilities from day one, so the position coach becomes a parent away from home. If the athlete was recruited by another coach who is not their position coach, that coach is also going to take a special interest in the athlete. Social health and a sense of wellbeing and belonging should never be an issue.

Every football program should educate its team on available support services in the event that they have confidential issues that might need to be addressed or some other issue that requires some form of professional assistance. I've seen athletes use these services very productively, and at times I've seen intentions that I might question. If an individual becomes disgruntled at some point in his career, he might overstate an issue to avoid some of the mandatory commitments he is required to meet. I believe that every coach wants the very best for his athletes, but if you have individuals who play the system, trust becomes an issue.

When you consider the attention paid to all aspects of wellness, you find it hard to believe that a young man's collegiate career could be somehow traumatic enough to cause him emotional or mental issues, but it does happen, and a coach needs to recognize it and refer it to a professional. It's no secret that many young individuals in today's society are medicated. As a strength and conditioning coach who deals with a number of athletes every day, it is very possible that you will encounter individuals who are prescribed a medication that helps them stay on task. Remember, they may forget to take those meds on any given day.

I prefer to consider what healthy individuals are expected to do well and then possibly draw conclusions over time regarding everyone's condition. We have a responsibility to recognize individuals who possibly need assistance. Hopefully, we can consistently recruit individuals who function well through all important domains of wellness.

Setting Expectations

Once we've done everything we can possibly do to find talented, committed and totally healthy young men, we must decide the direction we will take to influence them the moment they hit campus. At that point we are beginning to construct the "chief incalculable," otherwise known as the human dimension. Forty time, vertical jump, broad jump and other physical indicators should take a back seat to learning the nature of the traditions, standards, principles and values of the program. I believe that at the cornerstone of every program should be the understanding of integrity. The first team meeting should feature a definition and examples of behavior reflecting integrity.

Most people talk about honesty when they define integrity. Personally, I feel that the definition has to be very specific to the expectation of the organization. I also feel that it must be specific to the expectation of every department within athletics, and the university in total. Where honesty is concerned, the degree that a player is honest with himself when he looks in the mirror might be the most important characteristic to his success. He must be able to honestly assess his personal commitment to the demand, and that assessment also requires a sense of loyalty.

In the department of strength and conditioning, we require a commitment to the big four-- accountability, work ethic, self-discipline, and spirit. As far as I'm concerned, they all fall under integrity. In reality it becomes extremely simple for the athlete to understand. There are only two things that must be demonstrated--to show up on time and work as hard as humanly possible. Everything and anything else is monitored, coached and timed in a detailed manner. The athlete must have an extreme level of self-discipline to ensure a steady, linear and cumulative progression toward enhanced performance. That is a very specific type of integrity.

I truly believe that a collegiate football player has to place great emphasis upon listening and understanding detail. Mental mistakes will bring talent down to an incomprehensibly low place very quickly. In 2018 we talk about the inability of young people to focus and think deeply, because they are conditioned to multi-task. If I'm a position coach in this day and age, I'm forcing my position group to watch film until they are cross-eyed and I'm giving them written quizzes until they get hand cramps from writing. I have seen games lost countless times over the years by just a few, or maybe even one, crucial mental mistake. Players must have a strong level of integrity toward studying the game.

Similar to any operator in the military, the collegiate football player carries a tremendous responsibility to the other members of the team.

I think this is something that gets talked about a lot, but sometimes I question the presence of real commitment. There has to be significant observation and conversation about current levels of individualism. My feeling is that the coordinators for each unit should conduct a higher number of unit meetings. Here is where I must reminisce on my high school experience, along with the time I've spent around some old school coaches.

Anyone who has been around football has heard the expression "the film never lies." That statement is very true, and can be very embarrassing for those who get exposed in the presence of their teammates. I have been in meetings where players are called out in no uncertain terms, with the film repetitively rewound until the culprit produces some very specific answers toward how and why he failed his teammates, the position coach and the program. The position coach might be questioned as well. That type of meeting can be very intense. Possibly downright ugly.

People are very sensitive these days. You don't see much of this type of approach anymore, where someone is "put on the spot." Now it seems as though we are more concerned with learning from mistakes in a more civilized manner. I think it's quite clear that folks are getting fired for the mental mistakes of those who play the game in a mindless and unfocused manner. It also appears that the position coach or coordinator must assume the responsibility much more than the athlete. This creates a dangerous predicament, because the player feels less of a responsibility to his teammates. A mistake is not life or death to them; it is simply a learning experience. Military organizations would not be able to maintain our freedom with that same approach.

Another important characteristic that helps determine the specific integrity level of a collegiate player is courage. There are many situations through the grind of one's football career that require some type of courage. First, I think the speed of the game and the competitive level of Division I football is extremely demanding. You must have the courage to prepare for and play at that level. It is a grind. It requires individuals who are willing to grind. It is not always fun. Winning is fun.

Preparing For Impact

Secondly, the physicality of the game is also at a very high level. Athletes continue to become bigger, faster and stronger. Big objects moving very fast cause damage. There is a lot of discussion about concussions and the short and long-term effects of brain injury. It is real. I've heard the concerns of parents of young athletes. I know that I would not have changed things for myself, even though I suffered at least two concussions. Hopefully, we can minimize the risk moving forward. Personally, I would still assume the risk because of my love for the game. I just believe that you have to be 100 percent in or 100 percent out. Tentative individuals suffer injuries in this game. It cannot be played that way.

Sometimes, the luck of a team might result in the loss of several close games early in a season. It takes a courageous effort from the entire team when the chips are down. Getting back on track is a matter of believing in each other. One year we started the year 3-3 and might have been headed straight for mediocrity. Steve Logan gave a powerful "run the table" speech, and we won the rest of our regular season games and defeated Stanford in the Liberty Bowl. That took courage and resolve from everyone in the program. It was an expression of the kind of integrity that a team needs to persevere.

Once we are confident that our team is clear on the meaning and impact of integrity, we can begin to educate players toward the specific demands of collegiate football. One of the best ways to convey that objective is to inform the athlete of the number of common questions that might be asked by NFL scouts attempting to determine the individual's value to his organization. I've always thought it was a little crazy to answer questions from scouts that impact the monetary value of a human being's talent, habits, and character traits. Part of our job is to help our athletes get to the next level and get paid for the hard work and investments they have demonstrated through their career. The problem comes when individuals have talent, but poor character traits. It is extremely important that the young athletes entering a collegiate program understand that their behavior throughout their career could define their future. Poor behavior can be extremely costly, as it will impact the perceived value and commitment an individual might bring to an organization. The investigative process is going to go much deeper than the game tape. I have spoken to individuals who have been assigned to investigate potential draft picks on behalf of an NFL team. These individuals are not scouts; they have security responsibilities, and their questioning is very extensive.

Some of the primary concerns for the athlete should be directed toward the things people say when their name is mentioned. This seems pretty simple, but it is very true that from the time they step in the door, they begin to establish a reputation for themselves. This reputation will include their interaction with teachers, administrators, coaches, advisors, monitors, trainers, doctors, tutors, and the community or fan base. It is very common for all of these individuals to say the same things about these individuals, even though these people may not even interact with each other.

Some very specific suggestions to the athlete might be to exhibit coachability, compliance, toughness, commitment, great work ethic, social skills, consistency, durability, focus, passion for the game and a reputation as a self-starter. They will also need a clean record regarding any off-the-field issues or involvement with any type of drugs. I've seen very high levels of talent override some of the negative behaviors, but negative behavior is always going to be bring a cost. A player with high-round potential could end up as a free agent with labels to overcome, and that can be a hard road resulting in a short career. The word "character" gets tossed around almost everywhere you turn. When you talk or read about success, character as applied to collegiate football is very specific.

A Commitment To Excellence

In regard to what has been stated about trust, we should provide some information to the individuals entering the program that expresses the reasons they should trust the system. Players need to believe that winning is important to everyone from the top down. Facilities and state-of-the-art training equipment speak volumes. If that wasn't the case, we wouldn't be currently witnessing the millions of dollars being spent nationwide in those areas. I think players need to understand that the university and athletic department are doing everything possible to help facilitate the success of the program. Young people get very excited about some of the smallest things, things that are important to them. The first thing that Butch Davis did when he came into the UNC program was to get rid of the dingy white training shirts and worn training shorts and provide the players with three new sets of training clothes. It was like Christmas.

I've always thought there was something special about a good-looking team that looks sharp and dresses exactly the same. Of course, the athletes in today's arena love new uniforms, particularly if they are somehow unique. I can't remember any military organization that allowed individuals to dress differently. If a team receives clothing that looks good and has a sense of uniqueness, they will want to wear it. If everyone on campus has access to the same gear at the bookstore, it's not the same. Some people don't get that. If we want our athletes to feel special and appreciated for all of their hard work and hours they invest beyond the regular school schedule, then maybe they should look special. Just a thought. To me it is a simple formula. Athletes should understand that the success of the program begins with them. They certainly have a tremendous responsibility, and we want to provide them with everything they need to carry out the mission. We want them to know that they are winners and that they should take a winning perspective in everything they do in the classroom and beyond their collegiate experience. That process should begin with the freshmen orientation experience.

It's empowering to have a very high level of integrity and character specific to the needs of the collegiate football player and the belief that the player has every resource to get the job done. From the military perspective, I think back to the Vietnam War where we kept hearing about the flaws with the M-16 rifle and how it would frequently jam. I'm sure that government officials who learned about this issue felt terrible, but it was still too late to prevent the impact upon morale, not to mention the cost of human life. We don't have to consider the cost of human life in the college football scenario, but we do have to consider the life of the program as well as the resources that we need throughout preparation. The most important provision is probably adequate practice fields. This seems like a really simple issue. You need field space and a desirable surface. The problem occurs with poor weather conditions and lightning warnings, when athletes must clear the field and go indoors for the practice session. If you don't have an adequate indoor facility and you are unable to execute a productive practice during game week, you are in deep trouble with team readiness. Fans will never understand this. They just understand wins and losses.

The other factor that has presented itself to be crucial to success is nutrition. Nutrition is another component of wellness. It seems as if the issue has come full circle. Many years ago, there were schools that had dorms for athletes and what might have been referred to as a training table. Schools then moved away from that concept, and athletes adopted a lifestyle more similar to that of the general student population.

Recent research and improved knowledge toward the impact of what might be viewed as "super" nutrition for athletes has established a whole new approach. What we now refer to as a "training table" is a well-planned, fully funded program to optimize energy and recovery, thereby having a significant impact on gaining strength and lean mass. Also, there are now post-workout products and healthy snack foods that help with recovery and adequate caloric consumption. Athletes should be assured that they have the opportunity to practice under conditions that will optimize their preparation and also be able to eat to win. There is a give-and-take approach in effect throughout the total program.

The development of strength and conditioning facilities over the last decade has been nothing short of amazing. The size of a facility and the types of training that can be conducted within the facility continues to amaze recruits and their parents as they shop for the very best scenario to optimize performance. The trend has now moved back to racks and platforms, along with space provided for movement training and multi-jumps. The quality and appearance of equipment and flooring is somewhat incredible, along with the fact that manufacturers continue to upgrade functionality and the level of possible customization. The strength and conditioning program is a big-time selling point, and we should always be ready to communicate the reasons we feel that we do it better.

Since I grew up in the Pittsburgh area, I was a Steelers fan and I always listened to whatever Chuck Noll had to say, or anything he wrote, about the tremendous success he had with the Steelers. Chuck Noll believed in attitude. He believed that it was extremely important that his players maintained a positive attitude, with a high level of maturity, and stayed motivated. Perhaps Noll's most important view about attitude is the fact that he believed, as many of us do, that an attitude is contagious. It is contagious in either direction. Players need to understand this very early, because a negative attitude can be like a house fire; once that house fire reaches a certain point, all you can do is watch it burn. A great team attitude combined with talent is powerful.

I believe that a great attitude with mediocre talent and extreme toughness is also very powerful. I've seen it firsthand. Negative attitudes are self-defeating. You don't need to be very concerned with the opposition if you are beating yourself. Players must understand attitude. Coaches need to recognize it. A poor attitude in a military organization is not going to be tolerated by anyone. Anyone with a negative thought would do well to change that thought very quickly. Anyone I've ever met with a military background knows that commitment begins with attitude.

Setting The Bar High

As we progress forward and work through this initial education process, we should provide clarity at every turn regarding expectation. Expectation is a wonderful concept that we can be very specific to demand. Expectation and demand go hand in hand. Players are simply expected to meet the demand, but what they might not realize is that the demand is excellence. You might have players that have never been required to be excellent or were never subjected to the level of repetition, dedication or sacrifice that is required to achieve excellence. I always go back to my high school experience playing quarterback in a wing T type of offense. We might run the same play twenty-five times in a row in practice until it was perfect. I heard a vicious rumor that the Naval Academy might even exceed that level of repetition in the installation of its offense. Those guys are pretty smart. Interesting, if it's true.

When you live a football life for over fifty years you acquire a certain keenness toward the recognition of perfect execution. Having this ability influences you to accept nothing less than precision and purity in whatever it is you coach. Your perception becomes seasoned and your standard moves toward an elevated acknowledgement of performance that is uniquely symphonic.

The application of the word execution can be extended to offense, defense, and special teams. It can also be applied to the technical aspects of resistance and movement training. This is where we might think about the precision that we all have observed as we watch military organizations conduct marching and drilling with rifles. The U.S. Marine Corps Silent Drill Platoon is the most impressive demonstration of precision that I've ever witnessed. People stand in awe and scratch their heads about the machine-like movements that almost seem superhuman. Every football team should have an opportunity to witness it at least once.

Asking an athlete to study offensive or defensive schemes and make adjustments to multiple situations related to those schemes should not be too much to digest. When you see the possible level of perfection that is somehow achievable with young men in the U.S. military, it reminds all of us that discipline in execution is not only possible, but with enough focus and preparation can be nothing short of impeccable. As a strength coach, you have the opportunity to demand perfection in execution and require attention to detail every day. It starts with your group being on time and dressed properly. Everyone should look the same. Remember it's a team. If you start compromising any of these demands, I'm here to tell you that your team is moving in a losing direction. I can assure you that the U.S. Marine Corps Silent Drill Team doesn't tolerate individualism or mistakes; that's why they operate in a state of perfection. It might sound like a brutal demand to require that people achieve perfection, and we know it is not going to happen one hundred percent of the time. But when you watch the changing of the guard at the Tomb of the Unknown Soldier or the rigid behavior of a plebe and count the mistakes, you understand that there are consequences, and that's why mistakes are minimized.

Where collegiate football is concerned, we already know that the consequence of those mistakes is losing. When I observe an athlete who is unfocused and repeatedly disregards detail, you can be assured as to the direction the program is beginning to go. My point here is fairly evident. I personally believe that a team with discipline and minimal mental mistakes will be able to compete. The level of talent stacked on top of that will then take the team to new levels. The point is that discipline and exceptionally smart football must be the underlying foundation. If a coach attempts to use talent alone as a foundation for a program and compromises discipline, the result is always failure.

Military organizations believe that men must be built. A military recruit might be gifted with the eyes and natural ability of a sniper, but may never make it to a combat situation if he cannot achieve an acceptable P.T. score. The opportunity for perfection in execution is always going to be in direct correlation with consistently meeting the criteria of the organization. This has been established for many decades by every American military organization in their methods of teaching and training young recruits. If you don't believe this, then you have little faith in our military, and that becomes a danger to everyone.

As we feel confident about this status of the wellness domain of athletes entering our program and the understanding they gain of the vital principles necessary to success, they become ready for mental and physical preparation at a much higher level. The quality and progression of communication must be predetermined, simplified and structured, specifically in the installation of offensive, defensive and special teams programs. It is very important that the team members understand the price of mental mistakes and the advantages of deeper knowledge of the game. Anyone who has ever played the game can appreciate the value of repetition on the field; however, repetition on the field comes much easier with a clearer mental picture from repetition in the film room.

From a performance enhancement perspective, I like the concept of "installation" we use in football. Learning to execute resistance training movements requires a teaching process and a plan toward improving intermuscular coordination. It must include plans to install an extensive speed development, multi-jump, mobility and specific movement variation programs as well.

When developing a plan for a winning football program, the greatest consideration is getting young recruits off to a great start and preventing them from contracting any negative diseases that have been festering among the upperclassmen. Military organizations have a tremendous advantage in the fact that a recruit has no chance of being influenced in a negative direction. Any thought or action that has even a subtle appearance of resistance to the plan is met with a hard eraser and immediate reeducation.

Hitting The Ground Running

The U.S. Marine Corps has a specific plan for recruits that we can learn from. It begins with receiving week. They are in-processed in the middle of the night. They are issued gear, and of course experience the shaving of the head tradition. They are also strength tested to determine their readiness for training. This process reminds me of the young men we recently received to begin second session summer school. Even in 2018, many of them are "raw" regarding their training experience and ability to properly execute any aspect of training at a higher level. Their running posture is extremely poor. We knew that all of these young recruits had been excellent football players, and it was exciting to see that we still had a wide window of potential development. We also have a very extensive process of medical clearance for new team members. It has been somewhat alarming to me to see the number of athletes we discover to have physical issues that require us to immediately enter them into a modified program. I've never heard of any modified military boot camps, but I could be mistaken.

The first phase of training for the new marine includes the teaching of core values, including training in discipline through close order drills. I love the fact that discipline is learned through an intense form of physical training that teaches marines to be part of a team. I have believed in this idea for many years--let them experience and learn discipline through heartbeats and discomfort. An 8K hike builds unity, as do a dozen repetitions of perfect defensive pursuit drills. Marines also have to train in martial arts and swimming during their initial phase. Like the military, we can learn to ensure that we include every fundamental component necessary to future success.

I think that it is interesting that early in the fifth week of training the Marines conduct what they refer to as "team week." They take a break from the training and clean buildings and do laundry. They also get photos taken in their dress blues. It culminates with a 10K hike. The whole focus is to learn that you are part of something that is always going to be bigger than you. If we go back and look at the characteristics of the Z generation, we might realize how ingenious it is that after a four-week grind the Marines back off the physical component and emphasize the team concept. Learning to take care of your "house" is something that we talk about frequently in athletics. It is a team responsibility and an expression of taking pride in the organization and the facilities.

This phase of training also includes "grass week" and "firing week," during which Marines continue to be highly trained. Learning to master your trade, whatever that trade might be, must be part of the training. These two weeks of Marine Corps training include the mastery required for every Marine. Thus, the phrase, "every Marine a rifleman." Similarly, every football player must learn fundamentals. Blocking and tackling come to mind. As a strength coach, I might also include linear movement, postural integrity, acceleration mechanics and the ability to decelerate. It is significant to note that Marines go back to finish the week with a 12K hike—returning to a team activity.

It is interesting that in the first week of the third phase of training the Marines go into basic warrior training. After seven weeks, there are still basics that haven't been perfected relative to effectiveness and survival in combat. This process might be equated with the game situation preparation that is included in every team's total program. Every team rehearses its game plan, its special team schemes and what is referred to as "sudden change," with special attention to goal line and red zone situations.

The next week is focused upon testing. Marines are required to complete a combat fitness test and navigate the "confidence course" one final time. Another very important aspect of the training is that each individual is provided with a summary of his or her status and made aware of what is needed to improve. I don't think enough can be said for feedback. In my experience, the more in-depth feedback that an athlete receives, the more likely he is to focus on elevating his level of improvement. The Marines appear to have a very detailed system of testing the trainee throughout each phase of training.

The Marines place an emphasis on developing the individual attributes of each trainee, as well as consistently returning to team activities and events. Most people have heard of the culminating team event that grinds on for fifty-four hours. This "crucible" is designed to improve knowledge, skills, and values. Of course, those who complete this final event are awarded their eagle, globe and anchor, which symbolize the transformation from recruits to Marine.

When I look at the extent to which we train our military personnel and the effort that is invested in each and every recruit, it makes me extremely proud. It is no surprise to me that we are a free country. Any football program that could afford the time and possess the resources to train our young athletes at that level would quickly rise to a top twenty status and continue to improve from there.

We can only hope to bring awareness to improvements we might consider to develop a higher level of consistency and a stronger commitment to excellence within the hearts and minds of our athletes. I believe that taking lessons from the incredibly awesome military organizations we have developed in this country will make us a better society. We might consider some of the history and experiences that have influenced military organizations to arrive at their current methods to build the human element within a team.

Final Perspectives

Athletes and coaches who enter into a collegiate program should learn about the history of the school and the tradition of the program. Some traditions must be carried forward, and some might be required to change with the times.

We must go the extra mile in teaching and clearly defining the core values that represent the lifeblood of the organization. They are specific to the collegiate football experience. Members of the team must understand the serious nature of these values, and swift action must be taken toward any violations.

Like military organizations, collegiate programs must be built from the bottom up. This is unfortunate because the status of upperclassmen must be clearly defined, monitored and possibly changed until a new regime becomes solid. Everyone in the organization must respond the same way under duress. Combat readiness has to begin between the ears.

Leadership principles are always important. Collegiate athletes are challenged when we consider the actual degree of peer leadership occurring within a program. They need direction. They need to understand the various methods of influencing their peers without sacrificing friendships. For example, the leadership principle known as "bearing" requires you to represent your organization properly in the way you interact with the world. It encompasses your appearance and the choices you make reflecting your behavior.

There are countless ways of providing effective feedback to a developing student/athlete. Our ECU team completed self-evaluation worksheets, and they showed that many times individuals see themselves differently than the way they appear to others. It does appear to be true that this generation views their own behavior and performance in a more positive and productive light than their superiors. They might not realize this without feedback. As strength and conditioning coaches, we now have the ability, through technology, to provide a growing list of data to the athlete that alerts them to sleep patterns, nutritional behavior, effort, production of power, movement mechanics, etc. There is certainly a high degree of receptiveness to this information.

I found it very interesting that through the boot camp experience, the Marines always returned to a long team hike and finally the fifty-four-hour crucible--incorporating team events where individuals need to rely upon each other and work together. Football, of course, is divided into two units that compete against each other on a daily basis. We can always create events that stage them against each other, but it is also important to find ways to bring them together as a team. In week five of boot camp, the Marine trainees were doing laundry together and cleaning the facilities. It is a great change from the daily grind, and it serves to bring everyone together within a different scenario. I think we can learn from that. In my program we draft testing teams, and we also have an event at the end of the summer called the Gridiron Grind. These types of events promote esprit de corps.

The vital importance of toughness cannot be overstated. Some individuals do not believe that toughness can be developed, but I think that those perspectives are completely incorrect, even though there will be exceptions. From the time I was a young boy and put on my first set of helmet and shoulder pads, I discovered right away that I enjoyed collision. Likewise, I believe that others might discover right away that it's not for them. That is one aspect of toughness specific to football that might remain inherent. I believe that you can train your mind to go places that you never thought possible. Navy Seals do that for a living. Asking a football team to raise their level of tempo, focus and effort in the fourth quarter should not be impossible.

Let's remember that the human element is considered "the chief incalculable". The human spirit is the key to overachievement. I've seen a list of walk-ons earn scholarships and then sign NFL contracts. I've seen young men not have an opportunity to become a starter until their senior season. They were patient and kept working hard. They also signed NFL contracts. It's important to note that after the "crucible" was conducted and the men were awarded, they still had two weeks remaining. They were required to spend more time with their drill instructors and engage in additional training. The education process never seemed to end.

Semper Fi on the Gridiron

Strength and conditioning coaches spend an enormous amount of time and effort to get the most out of every minute afforded to them. Football coaches are under stringent guidelines during the competitive season. There is a high level of parity in Division I football. Teams are vulnerable to get knocked off on any given day by most teams on their schedule if they blink. Military organizations go the extra mile and then another mile to capture the hearts and minds of their recruits. That process beings immediately when their feet hit the pavement. They are broken down, pounded, reeducated, and finally embraced and welcomed into a brotherhood. Core values and leadership principles are the essence of what military organizations stand for. They are ready to sell out for each other at any given moment. Knowledge and physical conditioning are the secrets for athletes looking to become intrinsically motivated to the highest degree.

We now have strength and conditioning coaches contracted to train military personnel. The main issue they experience is attempting to convince the individuals they coach not to injure themselves by going too hard, too heavy, or too long. Accountability, effort, discipline and spirit are never in question. If we want to develop a winning program within the challenges of our current environment, we need to simply get everyone's head squared away and do it early. We need to ask ourselves how much effort we are investing on teaching core values and identifying individual issues within the roster. The Marines nailed it when they stated that they need to "identify the commonalities and shortfalls of each recruit relative to character, consistency and peculiarities."

When we discover a method to retain an entire recruiting class all the way to graduation, we will know that we have accomplished something truly significant. I have not experienced that through my thirty-year career. We continue to lose people to drug problems, academic issues, self-discipline dilemmas, discouragement and sometimes outright violations of the law. We continue to fail to recognize that losing players to various issues can completely decimate the depth and talent of a solid football team within a short period of time. We absolutely must change the process of the collegiate football experience within the first few months, immediately following entry into a program. I've heard about a sign at the entry of a military installation that reads "where the difference begins." Making a difference cannot occur unless we continue to scrutinize the process of cultivating the human spirit.

Physical Preparation

When we look at the parallels and similarities of objectives concerning the physical preparation of military enlistees and collegiate football players, it really comes down to making decisions related to the leadership theory concerning toughness. Some individuals currently focus on repeated sprint ability and the tempo of practice. It is obvious that the demands of a receiver are going to be much different than the demands of an offensive lineman and coaches must provide consideration for position specific demands.

Football is a game of movement for every position group. Through my career I have always included movement specific drills in my approach reaching all the way back three decades into "metabolic conditioning". This is where the position group leader would have a wrist band which would dictate sets of position specific movements on a "jog back". I've always believed this to be particularly effective for receivers and I still incorporate metabolics into our conditioning package.

Military organizations have traditionally focused on fitness levels and endurance. Running three miles for time and hiking ten miles is typical activity that seems to have been staple type of demands for all military organizations. Most strength and conditioning coaches in the tactical world of strength and conditioning have attempted to make changes in some of these traditions so that training has less of a catabolic effect concerning maximum strength development. Most coaches are in agreement that our military operators have a large window available for becoming stronger, faster and more athletic which would parallel the approach that we employ with collegiate football.

Those who might not favor a change in training military personnel might reference the fact that they do not want to sacrifice the mental and physical toughness derived from longer duration activity. This seems justified in my respects because there is a longer duration of higher levels of discomfort to adapt to in the field. There has also been well established tradition in the specific design of the challenges required to cross over into elite groups with very specific tasks. We can all agree that a stronger, faster and more fluid individual will be at an advantage in many situations, but tactical training is relatively new and military tradition has been established over many, many decades.

Because I believe that developing mental toughness is possible and because of what I've witnessed mentally tough young men accomplish, I still strongly believe in conditioning scenarios that demand it. I like shuttles at a distance of 300-yards with 25-yard increments. I like Dr. William Kraemers power unit for football which is 2 x 300, 10 x 40, 6 x 80, 10 x 20 and 2 x 300. We rest 2:30 between bouts. I like Peter Martinelli's progression of 200, 300, 400, 500, 600 that he used at Oklahoma. Of course, rest intervals and times were standardized by position. I like 300 yards around the perimeter of the field which I first witnessed with Walt Evans who was the strength coach for the Steelers. I like long hills like

Walter Peyton ran. To make the hill run even tougher, Walter found a soft surface that would absolutely cook your legs and hips. These types of conditioning protocols are tough. So is football. Some would argue that you only have to be so tough to have repeated sprint ability. I would probably agree with that. I don't think you have to be that tough to be a member of a football team with a very moderate conditioning demand. A 325 lb. man can make it through a football practice and a football game without having to be conditioned like a wrestler. What I am referring to is a mentality. A whole team that has been challenged at a high level over an extended period of time. A team that embraces hard work and is demanding of one another, whatever the task at hand. I believe that to be the key to a very powerful component of success.

I want to mention the photos again of the "military teams" throughout this book. They have been through incredible challenges and have been professionally trained in a manner where they just cannot get it wrong. Collegiate football programs have different strategies to develop a bond and a sense of comradery. I'm not sure anyone does it the same way. The Marines do it a little different than the Army and the Army does it different than the Air Force. The Florida Gators have a different tradition than the Miami Hurricanes. The key is that a team needs a tradition and I believe that every tradition needs American core values at the base of that tradition. To me, that's American football.

When we consider the way that we train our teams at the collegiate level and the way that our profession has evolved over the years, we find ourselves majoring in a 7-9 week training cycle. We have two mandatory developmental periods, one in the winter and one in the summer. If you have athletes who red-shirt, you might refer to the in-season phase of training as developmental for them. Typically those individuals are trained four days a week. A few years ago I met Major Jamie Farrelly USMC (Ret). We talked about the Marine Corp principles of leadership and how they might have a positive impact on the young men in our program. Major Farrelly set it up where different Marines with different leadership experiences came in and spoke to our team. I thought it was extremely impactful to our athletes. One of the leaders of a team talked about how he had been deployed six times and never lost a member of his team. He talked about being totally prepared for timing and circumstances. It was compelling. He opened some eyeballs. Each Marine talked about a different leadership principle and provided an example of uncommon valor that applied to each principle. We did this every Friday before the lift and the Marine would stay and watch us train as well as interact with the players. These men traveled three hours to spend time with us free of charge. There are other programs out there, but they are very expensive. I really appreciate what those Marines are willing to do to help our athletes.

When we consider the nuts and bolts of a nine-week program, we want to look at the factors that impact the fast twitch qualities of the athlete. We know that if we recruit and sign athletes who run fast and jump high that they have a chance to be a good player. That is a very simple concept. They will also adapt more readily to the training provided that the training is directed toward neuromuscular integration. We know that the neuromuscular system only understands intensity and can only be achieved by training fast or heavy. I've been training athletes fast and heavy for many years and I have always prioritized speed development in my program. I met a jump coach for track and field named Boo Schexnayder who is a highly regarded coach nationwide. As I listened to several of his presentations, I was elated to recognize that he was speaking my language but expressed it much more eloquently than myself. One factor that brought a big smile to my face was to hear that sprinting provided more tension in the muscle and connective tissue than any other type of training. All of us know that you have to train fast to get fast and that we should never confuse the body by training slow and long on a fast and short day. In fact, slow and long has no place in training collegiate football players. Running is divided into two categories. Those would be max effort speed and tempo. A max effort speed day is a typical day where we would extend the dynamic warm up to twenty or thirty minutes and follow that warm up with some type of progression of full speed work. The key being full speed work with adequate rest intervals providing full recovery. There are options to choose from related to resistance or assistance modalities. The key point here is that true full speed work with proper posture and force application does not require magic speed equipment. A coach needs to correct body position and cue important factors such as foot strike, arm stroke and stride separation. This type of training applied to military personnel might be considered initially mind bending since their bodies have been adapted to "long and slow". Every war movie I've ever seen has individuals sprinting somewhere with rifles or tossing a hand grenade and getting the hell out of there. I've seldom seen "jog mode" once the bullets start flying. Just in observation.

The second observation on a max effort speed day would be to perform multi-jumps otherwise known as plyometrics. This is where we would progress from the sprints to the jumps prescribed for that day. In our program, our jumps are categorized by intensity and number of contacts which we refer to as a plyometric index.

At this point we probably need to discuss the choice between a three day or four day lifting program. I've prescribed both types of programs every way possible over thirty years. One of the primary considerations is the recovery of the neuromuscular system. Optimal recovery might only occur through the implementation of a three day a week program. That would be lifting total body three days a week with placing max effort speed on those same days. The two days in between are dedicated to tempo work and position specifics. I will state at this point that I have also coached max effort speed in low volume, five days a week, earlier in my career with very positive results. I have also at times dedicated a day to drilling and technical aspects simply because I find collegiate athletes to have major issues with anterior pelvic tilt and posture through acceleration.

From a theoretical standpoint the progression of activity using a three-day program would be extensive warm up, sprint, jump, Olympic lifts, static lifts and post flex. Major lift might have a different focus each day. For example, we might strain through heavy weight with heavy bilateral movements one day a week. Another day would be dedicated toward velocity based training using tendo units to determine average velocity. We have also incorporated feedback with certain exercises whereby we observe average power or peak power. I've found it useful to average velocity with a block clean and box squat, average power with a push jerk or block clean and peak power with the power clean. These variations might be strategically placed in three week mini-cycles. I like to also focus on unilateral movement once a week as well. These exercise choices might include barbell or dumbbell step ups, rear leg elevated squats, single arm presses and pulls and kettlebell work.

Some coaches believe that a four-day split routine might not provide adequate recovery but I have found it to be very effective at times, particularly for developing strength as a priority and developing a higher level of lean mass with those athletes who must gain size. It is important to understand here that an individual can become more efficient in developing the neuromuscular system without developing size in the muscle. The point here is if you need to develop size in our athletes, you need a strategy for hypertrophy.

A four-day program can be split to be more effective. The Olympic lifts would be placed on a Monday and Thursday with pulling movements and the static lifts would be placed on a Tuesday and Friday with ancillary pressing movements. Max effort speed training would be placed on the same day as static strength because we will run and jump before we lift and prioritize the full speed work. Rep schemes for primary resistance movements would be from one to five with adequate rest.

On the other days when we are performing platform work we like to be fresh. We will run after the lift. These are short changes of direction and position specific days in the winter and tempo conditioning and position specific days in the summer. I also prefer to place posterior chain work on my pulling day in a four-day split routine. On both three and four-day programs we have evolved into a three-week rotation with primary lifts and since we expect to train for a total of nine weeks, we have three rotations.

I'm big on numbers and test results and I want to be able to determine if a team is developing explosive qualities. The way that I have determined that through the years is by incorporating my own power quotient. The quotient is an expression of both vertical and horizontal power. We take five values of vertical jump, plus three values of broad jump, plus one value of power clean and add them together. We then divide that number by 40 time. This formula has been good to me over the years in defining those athletes who come through the door with exceptional fast twitch qualities and more importantly it has indicated how effectively we are developing them in the program. This past summer I had right at forty athletes who power cleaned over 300 lbs., eighteen athletes with a broad jump exceeding ten feet and twenty-one players who ran a sub 4.60 forty time. This tells me that I have the results that I need to feel good about the program. Bench press and back squat results are still very important but the power quotient tells me that the strength is being converted into power. I have seen many players who demonstrate strength in the rack, however, they struggle on the platform and indoor track. Back in the days of wooden plyo boxes, these were the guys with scars on their shins. In today game we might still find these types of guys having success as offensive linemen, provided they are grinders, but they will struggle in any other position on the field. We must remember that in the game of football, the body is the weapon.

The latest version of the most effective four-day split routine is outlined in the illustration.

(primary movements in three week cycles)

Week 1

Monday

Pre-lift activation
Power clean (cluster singles)
Front squat (moderate resistance)
Pulling movements
Posterior chain
Grip / core
Post flex
    Week 2 - * power clean (peak power)
    Week 3- * block clean (.2 mps)
Tempo / conditioning run day

Tuesday

Extensive dynamic warm up
Max effort speed
2 chain bench press
BB incline press
Dynamic back squat (0.7 mph)
Pressing movements
Core/ neck
Post flex
   Week 2 - * 2 chain + 2 board bench press
         Dynamic box squat +double chain (0 .6 mph)
   Week 3- * 3 board press
         Dynamic box squat + bands (0 .6 mph)

Thursday (week 1-3)

Pre-lift activation

Power clean

Deadlift

Pulling movements

Posterior chain

Grip / core

Post flex

Tempo/ conditioning run day

Friday (weeks 1-3)

Extensive dynamic warm up

Max effort speed day

Back squat

Bench press

Push jerk

Pressing movements

Core/ neck

Post flex

Although the traditional protocols of boot camp throughout military organizations have been set in stone over many decades, it would be interesting to consider changing some of the training toward building strength and power as opposed to aerobic capacity and muscular endurance. It could be that things never change because a 150 lb. man who is in great shape can operate his weapon more effectively over a period of time because he has adapted to the duration of the grind. Those little guys from North Vietnam were pretty deadly. I don't think I would do much to change boot camp training but I do believe that military personnel can benefit from training that is very similar to the training we implement with collegiate football. This has now become more popular as tactical training seems to continue to grow. I think that it is still a situation where we take much more from them then they take from us, particularly what goes on in the preparation of the mind.

In summary, there has been some extremely important commentary toward the role and power of the human dimension in competition stated in USMC literature that is particularly enlightening, consider the following statements.

> *Like a living organism, a military organization is never in a state of equilibrium, but instead in a continuous state of flux, continuously adjusting to its surroundings. Command and control is not so much a matter of one part of the organization getting control over the other as it is something that connects all of the elements together on cooperative effort.*

> *"Opposition is not an inanimate object to be acted upon but an animate and independent force with its own objectives and plans.*

> *Warfare is dynamic interplay between opposing human wills.*

> *Friction is external or self-induced. Examples of external friction may be weather, terrain etc. Examples of internal friction may be a lack of clearly defined goals, lack of coordination, unclear or complicated plans and complicated technology.*

> *Training can never duplicate the friction of true combat. Remember that friction is both psychological and physical.*

> *There is an intrinsically unpredictable phenomenon known as the "fog of war". At best we can hope to determine possibilities and probabilities.*

> *Fluidity is the ability to adapt; to proactively shape changing events to our advantage as well as to react quickly to constant changing conditions.*

Train to eliminate critical vulnerabilities within your own organization.

Seek to attack the center of gravity of the enemy. Locate and focus on a critical vulnerability.

Determine which factors are critical to each enemy. Then concentrate our strength on their weaknesses.

Experience under fire reduce the mystique of combat.

As previously referenced, the Marines have a quote that encompasses the whole theme of this book. When I first read it I felt like much more needed to be said. It is that *"human nature is subject to the complexities, inconsistencies and peculiarities which characterize human behavior"*. These are precisely the factors that impact the performance of collegiate athletes.

2nd Platoon 1st Force Reconnaissance Company, USMC conducting desert patrol near Kandahar, Afghanistan. December 2001.

"Their drills were bloodless battles and their battles bloody drills"
- Josephus

By John Dailey

In an earlier chapter I talked about the rigors of Combatant Dive School. It's tough because it has to be. Diving into an enemy-held harbor is one of the most dangerous operations you can undertake. For that reason, you often hear the quote, "Plan the dive, dive the plan." It means you will never be in a better position to set yourself, and your team, up for success than before you start. That's the time to consider everything, think through the what-ifs and contingencies. What is the worst that can happen and when—not if—it happens, how will you respond?

On a combat mission there are a million things that can go wrong, and they start long before you leave the submarine or boat. We call this Murphy's Law—whatever can go wrong will. Murphy will stick his nose in when you have everything worked out and it's all going smoothly. And, the thing about Murphy is that he seldom travels alone. He brings friends, and they do their best to undermine the plans you've made and look for weak spots to attack. But, if you've thought through the problem, the worst thing that can go wrong, the most likely thing to go wrong, and all of the possible issues, when they attack you're not caught off guard. You're ready. You've expected it, and you know how to adjust. This is the reason that training can't be superficial or skin deep. It has to be repeated and repeated until you know the emergency procedures for a flooded mouthpiece in your sleep, because when it happens in twenty feet of black water you'll only have one chance to fix it. As my friend and mentor Pat Rodgers used to say, "Amateurs train until they get it right, Professionals train until they can't get it wrong."

The other reason that training must be tough is to build unit cohesion. If I have suffered with you, been cold and hungry with you, if I have seen you at your worst and your best, if I've carried your weight when you were tired, and given you mine when I was near a breaking point, I know what you can do. If I've celebrated with you at the birth of a child and mourned with you the loss of a friend, I know who you are and what you're about. I know I can count on you when the worst does happen and Murphy throws a monkey wrench into the plan.

In Force Recon we had another saying: "Everybody wants to be Recon until it's time to do Recon shit." When it's cold and wet and Murphy and his friends show up and they have you by the throat and they won't let go, that's when you make your money. That's what you're paid for. It's what Teddy Roosevelt meant when he talked about being the man in the arena. There are no time outs or do-overs. You will not rise to the occasion, you will default to your level of training. Make sure your training prepares you.

The Marines have a quote that has been previously referenced that encompasses the entire theme of this book.

If it was easy, everybody would do it.

John Dailey is a native of Hillsboro, Virginia in the Blue Ridge Mountains. He joined the Marine Corps at age seventeen, and over the next twenty-one years he served with Scout Sniper, Force Reconnaissance, and Special Operations units with tours in Afghanistan and Iraq. Although he left the Marines in 2008, he continues to train Marine Corps special operations personnel. He and his wife Tracy live in Hubert, North Carolina with their dog Max since their two children have left the nest. Dailey is completing an MFA in Creative Writing at the University of North Carolina-Wilmington.

WORKS CITED

Willink, Jocko. *Discipline Equals Freedom*, St. Martin's Press, 2017

Loehr, James E., Ed. D., *The New Toughness Training for Sports*, Penguin Publishing Group, 1995

Brooks, David. *The Road to Character*, Random House, 2016

U.S. Marine Corps. *Leading Marines (MCWP 6-11)*, University Press of the Pacific, 2005

U.S. Marine Corps. *Marine Corps Leadership (MCI 7404)*, Marine Corps Institute, Warfighting Skills Program, 1990

U.S. Marine Corps. *Warfighting (MCDP1)*, Create Space Publishing, 2013

Maxwell, John. *The 21 Indispensable Qualities of a Leader,* Nelson, Thomas Inc., 2007

Ricks, Thomas E. *Making the Corps*, Scribner, 2007

Lombardi, Vince Jr. *What it Takes to Be Number One*, McGraw-Hill, 2001

Didinger, Ray. *Game Plans for Success*, McGraw-Hill, 1996

Parcells, Bill with Jeff Coplon. *Finding a Way to Win*, The Doubleday Religious Publishing Group, 1995

Jakes, T.D. *T.D. Jakes Speaks to Men*, Baker Publishing Group, 2014

Graham, Billy. *The Holy Spirit*, Nelson, Thomas Inc., 2000

Johnson, Michael. *Slaying the Dragon*, HarperCollins, 1996

Gordon, Jon. *The Energy Bus*, Wiley, 2007

Lencioni, Patrick. *The Five Dysfunctions of a Team*, Wiley, 2002

Canfield, Jack. *Success Affirmations*, Health Communications Inc., 2017

Maxwell, John. *Developing the Leaders Around You*, Nelson, Thomas Inc., 2005

Bass, Bernard and Riggio, Ronald. *Transformational Leadership*, Taylor and Francis, 2005

Blake, Hugh. *Seven Principles of Transformational Leadership*, Red Wheel/Weiser, 2017

Rose, Robert, Ph.D. *Self-Awareness and Self-Discipline*, Rose, Robert Inc., 2013

Atkinson, William Walter. *Mastermind,* Yoga Publication Society, 1980

Lambertsen, Chris. *Navy Seal Mental Toughness*, CreateSpace Publishing, 2016

Maurstad, Nick and Holmstrom, Darwin. *Bristol's Bastards*, Zenith Press, 2008